The Devotional Life of a Pastor's Wife

Volume 2

By Various Authors

Copyright © November 2021. Revised edition, Volume 2 by Charlotte Claxton and other authors.

All rights reserved. No parts of this book may be reproduced or used in any manner without written permission of the copyright owner except for the use of quotations in a book review.

All scripture quotations, unless otherwise indicated, are taken from the Holy Bible. All rights reserved worldwide.

Scripture quotations marked (NKJV) are taken from New King James Version®. Copyright © 1982 by Thomas Nelson. Used by permission.

Scripture quotations marked (NIV) are taken from NEW INTERNATIONAL VERSION®, NIV® Copyright © 1973, 1978, 1984, 2011 by Biblica, Inc.® Used by permission.

Scripture quotations marked (MESS) are takes from *THE MESSAGE*, copyright © 1993, 2002, 2018 by Eugene H. Peterson. Used by permission of NavPress. All rights reserved. Represented by Tyndale House Publishers, Inc.

Scripture quotations marked (ESV) are taken from The ESV® Bible (The Holy Bible, English Standard Version®). ESV® Text Edition: 2016. Copyright © 2001 by Crossway, a publishing ministry of Good News Publishers. The ESV® text has been reproduced in cooperation with and by permission of Good News Publishers. Unauthorized reproduction of this publication is prohibited. All rights reserved.

All Scripture quotations marked (AMP) are taken from the Amplified Bible, Copyright © 2015 by The Lockman Foundation. Used by permission.
All quotations and definitions taken from another source have been clearly indicated and referenced in the appendix at the back of the book.

Exterior cover design by Natalie Decosta

Printed material by Frame Vector created by BiZkettE1 Freepik.com. This cover has been designed using resources from Freepik.com

Interior page design by Natalie Decosta and Sophie Holt.

Each testimony and story are true. To maintain anonymity some minor details have been changed.

The Devotional Life of a Pastor's Wife project lead by Charlotte Claxton. Foreword by Anonymous

Other authors include: Chantella Claxton, Sophie Holt, Hannah Sekimpi, Hannah Crisp, Natalie Decosta, Penny Boddy, Emma Ruzvidzio, Patience Makaka, Claire Mabey, Jacqui Wilkie, Rebecca Curtis, Mariah Brick, Becky Remigio, Heather Rice, Pam Kyriacou, Trudy Bennett, Kadi Ikutiyini, Joanne Dale

ISBN: 9798707950995

THIS BOOK BELONGS TO

....

....

For every woman who was, is or desires to be the wife of a pastor

Our prayer is that this book will further equip you as a Christian and cause you to fall in love with Jesus more and more

ACKNOWLEDGEMENTS

The Team aka 'The Armour Bearers'
Each of the following women were a part of the original WhatsApp group that inspired this book, without them this book would not have been possible. Every task that has been delegated to them has been fully embraced and efficiently completed, they have never let me down. Every devotion they have contributed has and will cause the reader to feel encouraged, challenged and inspired. Together we have fasted and prayed that this book would bless and revolutionise the life of a pastor's wife.

Chantella Claxton: Thank you for your consistency, words of encouragement and fantastic administrative skills.

Hannah Sekimpi: Thank you for your unwavering support, your time in formatting the manuscript and for your care of other pastor's wives.

Hannah Crisp: Thank you for being a listening ear and for making me laugh.

Natalie Decosta: Thank you for your tireless efforts on the design of the book; your skills have been paramount in this project. You are the reason it looks so beautiful. Thank you.

Sophie Holt: Thank you for the gorgeous artwork you contributed to the internal pages of the book. Thank you for picking up the phone (mostly late at night) when I couldn't contain my excitement about a new idea, devotion or when I had a question that I couldn't answer.

I thank everyone one of you for your friendship.

Doctrinal proof-readers
Pastor Daniel Crisp, Pastor Sam Holt, Pastor Adam Claxton, Pastor Lewis Claxton

These men willingly took on the important challenge of checking every devotion and testimony to make sure that every scripture fitted the thought. A time-consuming task on top of all that is required of them nevertheless they did it. Thank you.

Editors
Trisha Malone: A wonderful, faithful woman who desired to glorify God by willingly taking on the mammoth task of editing the 261 devotions and 52 testimonies. Although she had never edited before the team and I believed she possessed the skills to do it. We approached her and she at that point (during

Covid19) had been praying for the Lord to open a door for her to do something for Him; this was her answered prayer. God is good. She has been efficient and hard working. Thank you.

David Drum: David has been instrumental in the completion of this project; his editing skills have added the sleek touch to each devotion and testimony. We are so grateful for your lastminute.com interventions; they are remarkable. Thank you.

Proof-readers
Delphine Mensah and Cheryl Nembhard: Thank you for your diligent efforts in putting this book through the refining process. You've done a beautiful job.

Other
On behalf of myself and the team, we want to thank our families. Thank you for your love and prayers. There have been many periods during this amazing project when our minds and time have been consumed however you have been patient and released us. We thank God for you and love you to the ends of the earth.

Pastor Paul Boddy: For your support during this book and thank you for trusting us to do it.

INTRODUCTION

Hello, my name is Charlotte Claxton. I am a Christian, a mother, and a pastor's wife.

Who knew that 2020 would be a year that could change life as we know it, potentially for ever! I want to tell you a little about how the Coronavirus pandemic has changed my life and the lives of other pastor's wives around me, thus inspiring this book.

The rumours that the UK was going into lockdown were spreading around mid-February. If I'm honest (although I wished the circumstances weren't so horrific) I couldn't wait, I love being with my family. As I began to prepare for lockdown, stockpiling toilet paper (just kidding), school supplies and food, I pondered how this pandemic would affect our church. I considered the different circumstances the people in our congregation were living and dealing with (some with mental health issues, underlying health conditions, nurses, doctors, elderly, single mums, new converts) and wondered how was this going to affect them. *How was I going to engage with the ladies for potentially months? More importantly, how could I help them maintain a spiritual mindset and encourage them to stay focused on the Word and prayer?* The love I have for these ladies drove me to prayer, 'Lord you have to show me what to do.'

The Holy Spirit inspired me to invite the ladies to participate in posting a devotion on our WhatsApp group. I challenged them to use a scripture from their daily bible reading, write a thought to accompany it, and a prayer at the end if they felt necessary. It was a worthy shot in the dark if it meant we could all stay connected with each other and to Jesus. To my amazement, sixteen women responded. Words cannot express how insightful, encouraging, and motivating it was to read their devotions every morning during a pandemic; God used every one of them.

My mind also turned to pioneer churches, mainly pastor's wives. A church that is not yet established with core families and individuals could be detrimentally affected in a time like this. 'Goodness,' I thought, 'they're going to need a lot of encouragement, why not do the same with them but on a different forum?'

I invited five friends and all responded, a great result! Two and a half months into writing devotions the Holy Spirit challenged me to produce a book using the devotionals we had already written as the base for it.

How does the book work?
Instead of producing one massive book that has over 400 pages, we wanted to create something a little more manageable and less costly to purchase. We have therefore created four books that contain three months' worth of material, one for every season.

Days one through five consist of devotionals.

The sixth day is a testimony day, an account written by a pastor's wife about her salvation or experience on the harvest field.

The seventh day is an empty double page spread entitled 'Study/Sermon Notes' to encourage you to write your own devotion, study a scripture you have read in the week, take notes on a sermon, or journal what God is speaking to you about.

Bible in a year/Bible in two years
This book includes a custom made 'Bible in a year' and 'Bible in two years' programme at the top of every page like this:

Y1 - Genesis 1 & 2 / Y2 - Matthew 2 & 3

'Y1' refers to the first year where you will be reading through approximately half of the bible. 'Y2' refers to the second year where you will complete it by reading the other half of the bible. Alternatively, you can read 'Y1 & Y2' at the same time and complete the bible in one year. You can also print the full bible plan in pdf format from our website at www.pwdevotion.co.uk

The struggle to maintain bible reading is universal. Sometimes you must go back to basics; picking up your bible on the odd occasion will not carry you through. Therefore, we have produced a simple plan that accommodates all lifestyles, a plan that can get you consistently reading God's Word (without being overwhelmed). A plan that requires discipline yet inspires achievement. The plan works through one book of the bible at a time, alternating between the Old and New Testaments.

Additionally, in the back of the first book you will find a list of (whittled down) recommended reading that covers a range of topics which have helped many pastor's wives over the years. We hope this helps you!

Who are the authors?

The authors (in all four volumes) consist of thirty-three wives of current pastors, evangelists and missionaries, as well as those who have served in this capacity in the past. This mix was thought important to get both a current dimension and to glean from the women who have returned home after their time on the harvest field as their wisdom and knowledge bring a special aspect of insight and depth to the book.

The nature of the book

I'm sure you have already gathered that we are not professional writers, but we are women with experience, spiritual revelation and a desire to serve. In my initial pitch to invite these women to join the project, I understood that some would find it a breeze, some a challenge and others an impossible task. I stressed that their writing ability was not important (that's why we have editors) and it was in fact their insight and experience we desired.

Included in this book are devotionals and testimonies that are raw, insightful, unusual, deep, heart-breaking, witty, inspiring, uplifting, encouraging, and convicting, but I can assure you, all will leave you with hope and vision.

The purpose of this book

There are a handful of books written for the pastor's wife out there, but it seems, nothing quite like this. Over the years, having spoken to many pastors' wives, I have developed a growing concern regarding their personal relationship with God. You will invest in what you love.

Luke 10:27 (NIV)
He answered, 'Love the LORD your God with all your heart and with all your soul and with all your strength and with all your mind...'

For some pastors' wives it seems that their primary investments are elsewhere. Children, possessions and even the ministry, can consume you to the point that you lose a sense of urgency when it comes to having an intimate, active and a blossoming relationship with your Saviour. My prayer is that every pastor's wife, strong in the Lord or not, will dedicate themselves to seeking Him with all their soul, strength, and mind.

Here are a few objectives for the pastor's wife using this book

- Cause her to prioritise a devotional life of prayer, reading and studying the word of God; and as a result, change, grow, be restored, have fruit and be equipped for the good fight.

- Help her to understand and embrace the importance of her example.
- Inspiration for the harvest field.
- Clarity to this role she has been called to.
- Bring unity; we are all in this together.

'It's not always easy, but it's simple.'

This has become my motto in living my Christian life. I speak from experience when I say that I spent years trying to fight the 'duvet demon' to get up and pray in the morning. What I found is that fighting the flesh is not without effort, but it is a straightforward task. Fighting for the routine of praying and reading in the morning, coupled with studying the Word at a point during the week, has brought huge change in my life and I pray it will for you also.

Why pastors' wives?
Maintaining a consistent, close connection with God is a challenge for almost every Christian. It seems that once a couple of steps have been taken into the ministry, the devotional life can be one of the first things to be assaulted. The pressures build up, duties pile up, exhaustion sets in and before you know it, instead of feeling victorious you are left thirsty and dried out. I want to declare to you that this does not have to be the norm.

The pastor's wife is the silent server. Like a backbone, her ability to function practically and spiritually affects her husband, children, church, the community around her and potentially the world. My prayer is that she can operate consistently whilst soaking in the joys of life and the wonderous blessing of the Cross.

The proceeds of the book
100% of the profit will be donated to world evangelism.

Charlotte Claxton x

FOREWORD

At the beginning of the COVID-19 lockdown, I was asked to be involved in a new lockdown challenge: produce a devotion inspired by daily reading and post it on the WhatsApp group on my allocated day. The purpose was to help each of us dig deeper into the word of God, develop a stronger prayer life, and maintain relationships during that difficult period. My initial reaction was, 'Me? Really? Gosh, I don't know if I'm able!' I felt inadequate, but nevertheless I enjoyed the challenge, so I agreed to participate.

If I can be transparently and painfully honest before lockdown my mind was in shatters and so was my relationship with God. I had fallen into a deep pit. I was questioning my worth, wrestling with condemnation, and feeling entirely useless. Starting to creep in were thoughts of self-hatred and punishing myself, of being undeserving of everything I had. It got to the point where I didn't feel worthy to hold my child. I felt disbelief in my husband's words of love for me as I could no longer love myself. I felt so alone. The shame of these thoughts were unbearable, knowing they were ungodly, and continually saying to myself, 'Pastors' wives shouldn't think like this.' I felt like I was sinking and there was nothing I could do about it.

Little did I know God was fighting for me and He was making a way out. The challenge of writing a devotion every week caused me to read the Bible like never before. I experienced how relatable, encouraging, and challenging it was, and the more I read and prayed, the more I knew God and hungered for Him. Right there was the beginning of my deliverance.

When I look back, it's bizarre to think that I genuinely couldn't work out the solution because I *always* fully believed that Jesus was *always* the answer. Since this change in my devotional life, I can see clearly again. It is becoming easier to rationalise and look forward. I am slowly but surely growing in wisdom and discernment, and instead of falling apart at the first hurdle, I am taking a step back and assessing the situation and thus bringing it before God. I've learnt that God's timing is perfect down to the very second. He peels back layers bit by bit and gives you the resources to deal with all aspects of life. He is all we need and all we can depend on.

Matthew 10:30-32 (NKJV)
But the very hairs of your head are all numbered. Do not fear; therefore, you are of more value than many sparrows.

I received this verse from a preacher within the first few months of my salvation. Now, possibly for the first time, I believed it. Why? Because I have started to know God for myself on a personal level.

This book is a tool to help you develop or renew your own devotional life and draw you into a deeper relationship with Him. There is a direct correlation between seeking God and deliverance. The joy I feel now is no coincidence. I have yet to master the discipline of a consistent devotional life, but now I have the revelation I need to keep fighting for it because of the dimension that has been added to my life by viewing God as a personal God, a literal father, and a sincere friend.

Anon

April 1st – *Testimony*

Y1 – Ps 26 / Y2 – Ps 130

Salvation Story by Emma

When I really think about my testimony and all the miracles God has done in my life, it amuses me that I ever had the audacity to doubt God.

My brothers and I grew up with my mum being a single parent, and this led to real rejection issues and emptiness in my heart that progressed into a huge void. I tried all sorts of things to find satisfaction, throwing myself into education, relationships with boys, alcohol and marijuana. None of them managed to help and only left me with growing anger issues, shame, and self-loathing.

I started a new job and met a woman who had something different about her, an inner joy that I could not comprehend. At first, she invited me to all of the food events at her church, but the more I got to know her and her family, the more I wanted to know this Jesus that they talked about. She took me to an Alpha course where I decided to give Christ a chance. I am not someone who can boast of an explosive encounter that changed me dramatically in a moment, but I can say that the more of me I give to Jesus, the more of Him that lives inside me, and change is the result.

I have slowly moved along this road of faith and God has been with me every step. Not every issue has been conquered on the first try unfortunately, but He has never given up on me, even when I have wanted to give up on myself.

There is a peace that comes with knowing God that has enabled me to grow in a way I never thought possible. I now have a loving Father who never lets me down.

April 2nd – *Good Friday*

Y1 – Acts 13 & 14 / Y2 - Job 35 & 36

Isaiah 53:3-7 (NIV)
He was despised and rejected by mankind, a man of suffering, and familiar with pain. Like one from whom people hide their faces He was despised, and we held Him in low esteem. Surely He took up our pain and bore our suffering, yet we considered Him punished by God, stricken by Him, and afflicted. But He was pierced for our transgressions, He was crushed for our iniquities; the punishment that brought us peace was on Him, and by His wounds we are healed. We all, like sheep, have gone astray, each of us has turned to our own way; and the Lord has laid on him the iniquity of us all. He was oppressed and afflicted, yet He did not open His mouth; He was led like a lamb to the slaughter, and as a sheep before its shearers is silent, so He did not open his mouth.

After reading this portion of scripture, we can be left wondering, 'How can Good Friday be good?' Jesus died no ordinary death, being beaten, whipped, and crucified. But what man meant for evil, God meant for good.

1 Peter 2:24 (NIV)
He himself bore our sins in His body on the cross, so that we might die to sins and live for righteousness; by His wounds you have been healed.

The blood of Jesus has set us free! As Christians, we have something the Old Testament law could never give regardless of how strictly followed, and that is access to the throne of grace and the power to live in righteousness. Sin is a disease from which we can be restored because of the crucifixion. We must thank God for all that He has given us through Jesus' death and resurrection.

Lord, I can only imagine all that happened on Good Friday. Forgive me for brushing it aside. The pain and suffering you went through has given me so much and I cannot take it lightly. It is through your blood I have been set free and can say with assurance that heaven will be my home. Without you I would be nothing. Thank you! Amen.

April 3rd – *Trust Me*
Y1 – Acts 15 & 16 / Y2 - Job 37 & 38

Exodus 1 :16-17 (NLT)
When you help the Hebrew women as they give birth, watch as they deliver. If the baby is a boy, kill him; if it is a girl, let her live." But because the midwives feared God, they refused to obey the king's orders. They allowed the boys to live too.

The new guy on the Egyptian block became increasingly fearful because of the fruitfulness of the Israelites, so he commissioned Hebrew midwives to kill every newborn male they delivered. However, rather than obeying his instruction, these women showed tremendous courage by keeping them alive and protecting them instead.

How does this apply to us?

At the time Pharaoh was the most powerful ruler on earth and for us he represents the gods and cultural norms of our age. The midwives represent us because it is an important (and sometimes regular) part of our role to handle the most delicate things in God's kingdom. This includes the 'delivery' of new believers, the private heartaches of ladies, knowing details about people we'd prefer not to know, or even the frailties of our own husbands. What we do with what has been entrusted to our care will either stifle or enhance the spiritual lives of those around us.

Pharaoh's command was not obeyed 'because the midwives feared God'. They didn't get their reference points from the carnal chorus and earthly wisdom of their time because they were rooted in their relationship with the true King. This meant they could be trusted to give the right response under intense pressure. Their loyalty to the Lord brought protection and continued fruitfulness to the Israelite people.

God still desires to prosper His people today and looks for modern midwives who can be trusted to facilitate life around them.

Thank you, Lord Jesus, for providing me with trustworthy women as examples in the faith. They showed such courage and righteousness to protect your chosen people and I ask you to help me do the same. Help me not to damage, but deliver life. Thank you for trusting me.

April 4th – *Resurrection Sunday*

Y1 – Acts 17 & 18 / Y2 - Job 39 & 40

Mark 16:6 (NLT)
But the angel said, "Don't be alarmed. You are looking for Jesus of Nazareth, who was crucified. He isn't here! He is risen from the dead! Look, this is where they laid his body.

Those closest to Jesus, weary from observing His trial and torture, exhausted from mourning, and anxious about the persecution that yet may come, gathered to prepare the body for burial with the appropriate ointments. Their initial shock of seeing the empty tomb was quickly replaced by anguish that the Pharisees must have stolen the body. It was then that the angel arrived to bring this glorious message. Read it again. Now feel the true joy experienced in the realisation of His resurrection.

Romans 1:4 (NKJV)
And declared to be the Son of God with power according to the Spirit of holiness, by the resurrection from the dead.

This is the good news, not just for Easter, but for every day! The son of God was killed as the punishment for the sins of the world. Our sins nailed Him to the cross, our choices pierced His hands, and our forsaking of righteousness caused God to forsake Jesus as He entered into death. But that's not the end, hallelujah! Through resurrection He proved himself the one and only Son of God. He overcame death and through Him we can now have access to God and eternal life.

John 11:25 (NKJV)
Jesus said to her, "I am the Resurrection and the Life. He who believes in Me, though he may die, he shall live. And whoever lives and believes in Me shall never die. Do you believe this?"

Just as He died in the flesh, so we are to die to self and the lusts of the flesh. It's a privilege that we can live free from the bonds of sin forever and flourish in the will of God. Through His resurrection comes our resurrection into the Christian life of harmony with God, both in this life and the life to come. It was a glorious day then and it is a glorious day now!

April 5th – *Desire Wisdom*

Y1 – Acts 19 & 20 / Y2 - Job 41 & 42

The Bible has a lot to say about wisdom and how we should honour and pursue it fervently. Strong's Dictionary defines wisdom: *broad and full of intelligence, knowledge of very diverse matters, always giving the sagest advice, skill in the management of affairs.*[1]

Wisdom should be sought after: Wisdom *is* the principal thing.
***Therefore* get wisdom. And in all your getting, get understanding (Proverbs 4:7 NKJV).**

Wisdom begins with the fear of the Lord: **The fear of the LORD is the beginning of wisdom, and the knowledge of the Holy One is understanding (Proverbs 9:10 NKJV).**

Wisdom cannot be purchased: **For the price of wisdom is above rubies (Job 28:18 NKJV).**

Wisdom is priceless:
For wisdom is better than rubies, and all the things one may desire cannot be compared with her (Proverbs 8:11 NKJV).

God can give us wisdom if we simply ask: **If any of you lacks wisdom, let him ask of God, who gives to all liberally and without reproach, and it will be given to him (James 1:5 NKJV).**

We can grow in wisdom and knowledge through reading, studying, and being open to correction from God's Word: **And that from childhood you have known the Holy Scriptures, which are able to make you wise for salvation through faith which is in Christ Jesus (2 Timothy 3:15 NKJV).**

We can gain wisdom through listening to the wise people God has put in our lives: **A wise man will hear and increase learning, and a man of understanding will attain wise counsel (Proverbs 1:5 NKJV).**

We need wisdom to help us handle life with skill, to flourish in our lives as God would want. Being a blessing to our husband, raise our children, and be a friend one can trust. In all matters involving the church we must have wisdom because God has entrusted us. In all of life we need wisdom, it is the principal thing! Think about past experiences, what you have learnt along the way, and let God fill you with a fresh desire for wisdom.

April 6th – *On Guard*
Y1 – Acts 21 & 22 / Y2 – John 1 & 2

Ephesians 6:11 (NIV)
Put on the full armor of God, so that you can take your stand against the devil's schemes.

The armor of God is a metaphor in the Bible that reminds Christians about the reality of spiritual battle and describes the protection available to them. The enemy is powerless over us unless we believe his lies and accept his schemes. One of those weapons used against us is fear, something I never had a problem with until we became missionaries.

When we moved to China several incidents unnerved me, including witnessing three accidents involving E-bikes in the space of a week, one of which I had to administer first aid. I also read about some horrible escalator and lift accidents because health and safety regulations are a running joke in this country. I suddenly felt overly protective over our three children. The thought came, 'You better just accept that one of your children is going to die here.' Obviously, it was a flaming arrow from the enemy, but it seemed so logical and true. I knew I was dealing with 'schemes of the enemy' but over time I had subconsciously accepted those lies. I even began to notice an emotional distance between me and my children, almost like my heart was preparing for the blow. The coping mechanism of disassociation caused me to disconnect from my emotions, surroundings, and at times caused great anxiety.

2 Corinthians 2:14 (NKJV)
Now thanks *be* to God who always leads us in triumph in Christ...

I realised the need to stand against this strategy and put on the armor of God. My husband and I renounced the spirit of fear and confessed that God gave us power, love, and a sound mind (2 Timothy 1:7). This fear had no right to be here! Once we cast it out in the name of Jesus, I felt my peace was restored. Now, five years later, I can tell you, God has protected us and kept us all healthy and safe. He is faithful!

April 7th – *Testimony*

Y1 – Ps 27 / Y2 – Ps 131

Salvation Story by Patience

I grew up going to a Roman Catholic church that my dad served in even before he married my mum. I must say we were treated very well there and, in fact, it felt like family. From a young age, I was aware of heaven and hell and knew that sin would separate me from God. I was open and hungry for God and did experience His love whilst in the church, getting confirmed while I was still in primary school.

At the age of 20, I moved to the UK to pursue my studies at De Montfort University in the city of Leicester. I attended church, but it was quite different and did not feel like the same Catholic Church. It was boring, lifeless, and I couldn't really understand their preaching. I was beginning to feel distant from God and was really missing my church back home. I felt guilty for feeling that way and cried out to God to help me. Thankfully, it was not long after that I went over to my friend's house and met his cousin who invited me to come to his church. I decided this might be an answer to prayer, so I went to check it out. Whilst there, the preacher challenged the congregation about sin, repentance, and being religious in practice, but far from God. The message was very clear! I knew in my heart that he was talking to me and that I had to address these issues in my life. So I prayed, and gave my life to Jesus Christ, never looking back. I realise now that what I was missing all along was a true, dynamic relationship with God.

In 2013, my husband and I were announced to go and pioneer a church. We thank God for good and faithful saints, and the many more He will bless us with, in the future. I always strive to love people and create that same sense of community and acceptance in which I grew up.

My testimony may seem simple, but I want you to know that there are millions of people out there like me who are in desperate need of revelation and redemption. Please don't write them off, feel intimidated or underestimate their need because they look like they have it all together (academically, socially, physically, spiritually). Make every attempt to reach them in whatever way you can, you never know you could be working with a future pastor's wife.

April 8th - *Study & Sermon Notes*

Y1 – Ps 28 / Y2 – Ps 132

April 9th – *The Stash*
Y1 – Acts 23 & 24 / Y2 – John 3 & 4

1 Kings 17:16 (NIV)
For the jar of flour was not used up and the jug of oil did not run dry, in keeping with the word of the LORD spoken by Elijah.

The widow at Zarephath had a plan: use her last little stash of oil and flour to bake a cake for herself and her son before giving in to starvation caused by a famine in the land. Elijah the prophet asks her to give him the cake instead with the promise that she would have enough to eat until the famine was over. Although undoubtedly nervous, she complied and subsequently saved herself and her son from death. Her obedience changed her fate.

I was once challenged in a sermon about my stash. Although my husband and I share all of our money, we had agreed that I would have a little cash set aside from selling my handmade goods. It was in no way a large amount, but I did feel that this money was *mine* because I had worked really hard to earn it. Despite knowing that Jesus was asking me to give it (all of it), I felt anxious and conflicted in my spirit.

When Elijah asked the widow to give all she had left to meet a need, she obeyed. She stepped into God's plan and laid aside her own ideas. As pastors' wives we face challenging decisions when it comes to money. Finances aren't always available in excessive amounts, but God wants us to be generous, plan how we spend, and to be wise. Money is a reflection of who we are; it is us in spendable form.

Would you give all you had to God if He asked for it? Are you fully surrendered in your will and your finances to the Lord?

In faith, I gave my stash and today have seen incredible blessings flow from that sacrifice. God owns it all and doesn't need our money, but He loves it when His children are obedient.

April 10th – *Day & Night*
Y1 – Acts 25 & 26 / Y2 – John 5 & 6

Psalms 1:2-3 (NKJV)
But his delight *is* in the law of the Lord, and in His law he meditates day and night. He shall be like a tree planted by the rivers of water, that brings forth its fruit in its season, whose leaf also shall not wither; and whatever he does shall prosper.

Meditate: *to reflect; to moan, to mutter; to ponder; to make a quiet sound such as sighing; to meditate or contemplate something as one repeats the words.* Hagah represents something quite unlike the English "meditation," which may be a mental exercise only. In Hebrew though, to meditate upon the Scriptures is to quietly repeat them in a soft, droning sound, while utterly abandoning outside distractions. From this tradition comes a specialized type of Jewish prayer called "davening," that is, reciting texts, praying intense prayers, or getting lost in communion with God while bowing or rocking back and forth. I thought this was interesting because when I learned how to pray I naturally started to rock back and forth.[1]

I had always associated the word meditation with eastern religion and new age chanting. In reality, these are sad copies of the true original practice of biblical meditation. Of course, we learn through studying our Bibles, but when we meditate on one or two verses, we are opening our hearts to His revelation. It is not just memorising, but repeating them audibly, which plants them into our hearts. Meditation produces an active faith that applies God's promises, renews our minds, and transforms our lives. Read Joshua 1:8-11 and you will see that meditating on God's law and promises is the key to gaining victory in future conquests and taking personal responsibility.

Don't leave the words on the page. Nourish your spirit by being still, focussing on the word, and speaking it over your life. For many years I did not realise the transforming power of meditation, now I implore you to develop this so you can experience a fruitful and prosperous future.

April 11th – *Psalm Sunday*

Y1 – Acts 27 & 28 / Y2 – John 7 & 8

Mathew 21:7-9 (NKJV)
They brought the donkey and the colt, laid their clothes on them, and set *Him* on them. And a very great multitude spread their clothes on the road; others cut down branches from the trees and spread *them* on the road. Then the multitudes who went before and those who followed cried out, saying: "Hosanna to the Son of David! 'Blessed *is* He who comes in the name of the Lord!' Hosanna in the highest!"

As Jesus enters Jerusalem on a donkey, He is fulfilling prophecy[1] and the hopes of many in Israel who have anticipated the coming Messiah. The crowds, most of whom were visiting Jerusalem for the Passover, had heard or seen the miracles of Jesus. Stirred, they laid garments and leaves like a carpet on His path, a sign of great honour and respect, rightfully praising Jesus as Lord and shouting 'Hosanna,' which translates 'save us now.' This was a joyous event filled with praise, song and dance, yet within a week the situation changed and the same crowd cried out, 'Crucify Him!'

Luke 23: 20-21 (NKJV)
Pilate, therefore, wishing to release Jesus, again called out to them. But they shouted, saying, "Crucify *Him*, crucify Him!"

To worship and exalt Jesus as Lord is easy when there are miracles, the crowds are joining alongside you, and things are joyful. However, how quickly our emotions turn when the miracles stop and the crowds depart. *What will your response be? Will you be one of the faithful few who remain steadfast?*

Luke 23:27 (NKJV)
And a great multitude of the people followed Him, and women who also mourned and lamented Him.

Lord, I strive to exalt you in every area of my life. Reveal to me how to develop faithfulness so that I would cry 'Hosanna' in triumphant times or when persecution arises. Let my conviction for you as my Lord move me to glorify you in all circumstances. Amen.

April 12th – *Jehovah Rapha*

Y1 – Lev 1 & 2 / Y2 – John 9 & 10

Exodus 15:26 (NLT)
He said, "If you will listen carefully to the voice of the Lord your God and do what is right in His sight, obeying His commands and keeping all His decrees, then I will not make you suffer any of the diseases I sent on the Egyptians; for I am the Lord who heals you."

The children of Israel had escaped Pharaoh's army in the Red Sea and subsequently praised God. However, after travelling in the desert for three days with no water, they began to complain. When they finally did find water, it was undrinkable, until the Lord performed a miracle. The water being healed was a picture of the spiritual transformation God had done in them; He then makes the promise that He is Jehovah Rapha, the God who heals.

The children of Israel physically needed water, but spiritually they needed their faith to be increased, mentally an assurance of God's provision, and emotionally to know God can heal and keep them despite their circumstances.

As sinners, we suffered the physical, spiritual, mental and emotional consequences of sin. Now, as believers, not only can God heal us physically, but we are forgiven, accepted into the kingdom, and can access the full healing power of Jehovah Rapha. God can heal us from the internal ailments and scars brought about by the heartbreak and sufferings of living without Him. He can also heal us from any ongoing pain we experience.

Just as the children of Israel were in need of healing physically, spiritually, mentally, and emotionally, so shall we throughout our Christian walk. In these times, let's remember we can call on our God, Jehovah Rapha, the God who heals.

Acts 4:29-30 (NLT)
And now, O Lord, hear their threats, and give us, your servants, great boldness in preaching your word. Stretch out your hand with healing power; may miraculous signs and wonders be done through the name of your holy servant Jesus."

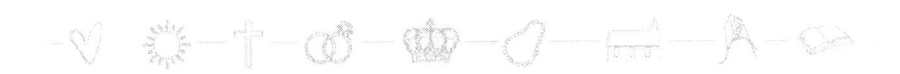

April 13th – *Ah, Patience!*

Y1 – Lev 3 & 4 / Y2 – John 11 & 12

Romans 8:28 (NKJV)
And we know that all things work together for good to those who love God, to those who are the called according to *His* purpose.

Romans 8:28 (MSG)
He knows us far better than we know ourselves, knows our pregnant condition, and keeps us present before God. That's why we can be so sure that every detail in our lives of love for God is worked into something good.

How have you learnt to deal with the challenges and hardships that the ministry brings?

The enemy will throw fiery darts in your life and ministry to discourage you and cause you to grow weary. Going through pain or suffering is no fun, but we have a promise that God is at work for our benefit. Like a pregnant woman about to give birth, who experiences tremendous labour pains and suffering, the result is something astonishing and beautiful.

Setbacks and disappointments are inevitable. Perhaps you faithfully invest in the people of your church, loving, trusting, serving, and pouring your heart into them, only to have some leave. For no apparent reason they disappear and you are left to wonder what happened. It is heart-breaking! We might be running around like headless chickens trying to balance marriage, family, work life and ministry commitment. It can be overwhelming!

Galatians 6:9 (NIV)
Let us not become weary in doing good, for at the proper time we will reap a harvest if we do not give up.

Don't quit. The harvest is coming! You are called by God, for God, and are part of His plan and purpose! Take time right now to meditate on His promise, 'all things work out for good to them that love God.'

Lord Jesus, I thank you for saving me from my sins. I know you have a plan and purpose for my life; help me not to feel discouraged and to understand that you are training me to fulfil Your will on the earth. Amen

April 14th – *Testimony*

Y1 – Ps 29 / Y2 – Ps 133

Conflict Resolution by Anon

Relationships with our brethren, headship and family bring challenges and situations which hopefully will change us into becoming more Christlike. Interaction with people will force you to your knees, bring tears of sorrow and joy, produce introspection, and lifelong friendships. It will also reveal whether we can live out what we read and preach to others.

However, I had a deeper and even more challenging lesson to learn when I realised that God would use conflicts with our fellow labourers to change us. This shocked me! After all, we are fellow soldiers fighting together in the same battle; on a mission with the same vision to reach the world for Jesus. This is the arena God often uses to change His ministers.

Over several months, I noticed when visiting a fellow pioneering church that it seemed I was being shadowed. Then, at a Bible conference, after a morning seminar, the pastor's wife of this church asked me to escort her into our headship's office. A little baffled, I followed her thinking that perhaps she needed support. To my surprise, then shock, the meeting was about me and my actions. The pastor had spoken to my husband several months before about me calling the saints in their church and giving advice. My husband never mentioned this to me as he knew it was not true. I was speechless. Was I this person they were describing who was trying to destroy another couple's ministry? I certainly did not recognise any of the accusations in me. Anyway, I apologised to make the peace. My co-labourer was deeply hurt and upset, but seemed to find a little relief from my apology. I was instructed not to phone or speak to any of their congregation and warned that I was being monitored.

As I walked out of the office, dazed and confused, I met one of my dear friends who instantly saw on my face that something had happened. We walked around the outside of the conference hall several times, allowing me time to digest what had just been said. Only in that safe space with the reassurance and love of my friend did the tears begin to flow.

It probably took a year to recover from that encounter. Six months consisted of trying to do a personality makeover and beating myself up for being too loud, interfering and opinionated. I was tormented by the question, 'How many more people viewed me like this?'

A sense of shame caused me to question the person I thought I was and made me feel my own judgement could not be trusted. Bitterness began to take root, distrust towards my fellow labourers, suspicion of headship, and introversion because, 'I must be the talk of the fellowship!'

Finally, I looked deep into my heart, inspected my motives, and sought out God's opinion on the situation. I hid in the comfort of my dear friends who walked the path of restoration with me. Eventually, I was able to thank God and forgive the people for what had happened.

Pastor's wife, God has made you as you are and He has all things under control. Conflict needs to make you, not break you, nor keep you from cultivating relationships with your husband, others in the ministry, friends, and God.

April 15th - *Study & Sermon Notes*

Y1 – Ps 30 / Y2 – Ps 134

April 16th – *Navigating Emotions*

Y1 – Lev 5 & 6 / Y2 – John 13 & 14

Acts 13:49-52 (NKJV)
And the word of the Lord was being spread throughout all the region. But the Jews stirred up the devout and prominent women and the chief men of the city, raised up persecution against Paul and Barnabas, and expelled them from their region. But they shook off the dust from their feet against them, and came to Iconium. And the disciples were filled with joy and with the Holy Spirit.

Paul and Barnabas were falsely accused, resulting in persecution against them and the work of the gospel. However, they chose not to take it personally, they maintained the ability to be objective and then move on to the next area where they had a positive impact. No doubt, we have all experienced words spoken against us, our husbands, the church, but how we handle those is vital. We can undermine our faith and future by being angry, upset and bitter, or we can consciously make an effort to let go of the hurt and move on.

To be objective can be defined as a person (or their judgement) not influenced by personal feelings or opinions in considering and representing facts.[1] Paul and Barnabas knew God was with them and working for them. Their hurt or frustration didn't change that.

For example, during our time in the ministry, we have watched other churches excel, have breakthroughs, get buildings, and see miracles whilst our experience has been quite the opposite. It was so easy to allow hurt, jealousy, frustration and anger cloud my thinking, when in reality I was only hindering myself. God has helped me to be genuinely happy for people and now I thank God for all He is doing in their ministries. The fact is, no one has it easy and everyone has their own struggles, you just might not be able to see them.

Lord, I ask you to help me control my emotions and maintain a balanced perspective. Fashion my character to be like Yours, undeterred by the circumstances that surround me. Amen

April 17th – *Memory Loss*
Y1 – Lev 7 & 8 / Y2 – John 15 & 16

Psalms 103:2 (NKJV)
Bless the Lord, O my soul, and forget not all His benefits.

Our Wednesday night church service was finished, and after chatting with our congregation I said to my wonderful husband, 'Babe, I'm going home now to put our daughter to bed, would you mind getting our son from the nursery on your way home? He is fast asleep' He happily agreed. About forty-five minutes later, he walked in the house, locked eyes with mine, and bolted back out the door saying, 'I'll be back in a minute!' Yes, that's right, he had locked up the church and left our son in the nursery. Fast asleep.

I am sad to say that my memory is not as it used to be (and I am only twenty-eight years old); forgetfulness is almost inevitable as the years go by and indeed there are many reasons for it. However, there are events, truths and convictions that we must never forget.

There are some things the Bible asks us to keep in mind. Remember the Sabbath.[1] Remember Jesus in the breaking of bread.[2] Remember 'the days of old'[3] (where you have come from). Remember Lot's wife.[4] Remember you were once slaves in Egypt.[5] Remember my chains[6] (Paul is asking the church to bear in mind those who are persecuted), and remember the deeds of the Lord.[7]

In addition to these major things there are many little, but important details of people's lives that are helpful for the pastor's wife to remember. Remember names. Remember people's food allergies or special diets so you can cater to their needs when they have dinner at your house. Remember people in prayer. Remember important events in their lives. Remember to ask them how their interview/ holiday/ doctor's appointment went. I'll let you off the hook a moment and say that to remember all of these things for every congregation member is impossible, but the personal touch goes a long way and will demonstrate love and care.

Make it your task today to remember what the Lord has done, no matter how insignificant.

Lord Jesus, I acknowledge how important it is to remember life's events. I'm asking for your help not to dull my senses by mindless pursuits, but to desire and develop a better memory. Most of all, help me remember Your Word that gives much needed spiritual strength for each day. Thank you! Amen.

April 18th – *True Friend*
Y1 – Lev 9 & 10 / Y2 – John 17 & 18

Proverbs 18:24 (NLT)
There are "friends" who destroy each other, but a real friend sticks closer than a brother.

After I got married, I was surprised and interested at how the dynamic with my friends changed for better and worse. Husbands are wonderful, but sadly due to their lack of ability to paint nails, shop 'til you drop, talk for hours, cry on demand and drinks copious cups of tea, they simply cannot be expected to replace our girlfriends! Friendships are a huge part of our lives and it is crucial we maintain them.

Within the first few months of ministry, I dreadfully missed the friendships in my mother church. We left a bustling congregation and pioneered from scratch. The two were worlds apart. Sometimes you can be surrounded by people and still feel alone. I believe Jesus understands these seasons, having found himself alone prior to the crucifixion, yet surrounded by people. However, Jesus was speaking to His Father, He wasn't alone. He confided in the One who would never leave Him or forsake Him.

In moments of loneliness you need to depend on the Lord to meet your intimate needs. *When things happen in life, do you turn to people first or do you take it to the Lord? Do you get your identity and affirmations from those around you or from the Word of God?*

Once we entered ministry, I had to change how I depended on God to meet my need for friendship. I learnt I had to build new relationships. I saw God move in the supernatural and bring in women to pray with and be encouraged by. Whether friends are near or far, be creative and reach out, but don't let it replace the most important friendship you have with Jesus.

Father, I feel desperately lonely but I know that I am not alone. I will not listen to the lies the enemy feeds me but remember to speak my heart to You. I ask You to fill me with the joy of the Holy Spirit. Thank you, in Jesus name. Amen.

April 19th – *Run ... Run!*
Y1 – Lev 11 & 12 / Y2 – John 19 & 20

Exodus 4:10 & 13 (NKJV)
Then Moses said to the Lord, "O my Lord, I am not eloquent, neither before nor since You have spoken to Your servant; but I am slow of speech and slow of tongue." ...But he said, "O my Lord, please send by the hand of whomever else You may send."

I felt an affinity with Moses' reaction to his calling. I always knew that my husband was called to preach, but I ran from this calling using a range of excuses. I lacked peace because being outside of God's will is not a comfortable place to be.

Part of my problem was that I didn't feel good enough to be a pastor's wife. In my mind, it required a level of perfection that I could never live up to. I thought perhaps my past failures, which had always been a tool to connect with people, would be an albatross that would somehow hinder my husband's ministry.

I love God's response to Moses fear.

Exodus 3:14 (NKJV)
And God said to Moses, "I AM WHO I AM." And He said, "Thus you shall say to the children of Israel, 'I AM has sent me to you.'

In Moses' uncertain 'who am I?' comes God's certain 'I AM!'

Moses was also a sinner with a past. God doesn't require us to be flawless, just willing. Then, 'I AM' will allow our "who am I?" to flourish in the task He has set for us.

2 Corinthians 12:9 (NKJV)
And He said to me, "My grace is sufficient for you, for My strength is made perfect in weakness." Therefore most gladly I will rather boast in my infirmities, that the power of Christ may rest upon me.

Do you trust the Great 'I AM' to make up for your shortfalls? Think of a time when you felt ill-equipped to carry out a task but 'I AM' brought you through it. 'I AM' is present tense, meaning, He is with you right now!

April 20th – *Subtle Resentment*

Y1 – Lev 13 / Y2 – John 21

Job 2:9 (NIV)
His wife said to him, "Are you still maintaining your integrity? Curse God and die!" He replied, "You are talking like a foolish woman. Shall we accept good from God, and not trouble?" In all this, Job did not sin in what he said.

Horrible, devastating circumstances beyond what most people can even imagine; Job had suddenly lost all his property, livelihood, and the worst of all, his beloved children are dead. On top of all this, Job is covered with boils from head to toe and they itched so bad he used a piece of broken pottery to scrape himself. Not a pretty picture. Nevertheless, he does not 'sin in what he said' through all of this, which is a miracle. Through God's grace and humility, Job can see that life is not always fair. It gives both good and bad, and that complaining and cursing God is not helping anybody. Job is truly an example to all of us.

However, if we zoom in on Job's wife, she is having a breakdown and questioning why Job seems to be coping while she's falling apart at the seams. Where is God? Why doesn't Job just curse God and die? After all, living like this is worse than death.

Do we sense a hint of resentment in Job's wife? A 'bitter indignation at being treated unfairly,'[1] maybe?

Let's bring it a little closer to home... have you ever thought, 'No one sees me! Lord, if You don't care about my sacrifices, then here's my resignation!'

Can you imagine yourself in this situation? How would you respond to God? Is there anyone you resent at this point in time?

Job 21:25 (NKJV)
Another man dies with bitterness of his soul, never having eaten with pleasure.

Resentment achieves nothing, it will rob your joy, and leave you feeling unsatisfied. Life isn't fair, but we must keep a righteous perspective. Life can dole out heavy blows, pastor's wife or not, but we can't let circumstances hinder our personal walk with the Jesus. Lay down your resentment before God, let Him restore your mind and give you a new perspective. In the end, Job was blessed. It is a season, but through it all He is faithful.

April 21st – *Testimony*

Y1 – Ps 31/ Y2 – Ps 135

Life's changes by Anon

Over the years I have listened to the various life experiences of our pioneers, some funny, some uplifting and some distressing. As for my personal experience, serving as the wife of a pastor, I can honestly say I loved it. I was driven for souls, fired up spiritually, served and greatly enjoyed our congregation. Seeing lives transformed completely thrilled me. After all, before my husband and I accepted Christ, our own marriage was in ruins and our hearts utterly broken. Jesus restored our family. To have the opportunity to share that same life-transforming salvation message with our new community was awesome. Our children had grown up and moved out, and we were able to give everything. I treasured supporting my husband. We were in the will of God.

I wasn't to know however that this dream life of mine was all about to change. After years of service, exhausted and burnt out, my husband made the decision to return to our mother church. I understood his reasons and I understood it was the right thing to do, but I struggled desperately to adapt. We retuned during the covid 19 pandemic. Our country imposed strict isolation measures and we were unable fellowship with anyone. I felt lost and useless. I switched off to the world. I couldn't find my place anywhere. Vision impaired. Passion diminished. The mind assaults were so intense at times that all I could do was cry. What was I to do?

Like a stubborn donkey, I dug my heels in and refused to let the enemy derail me. I had to search my heart, forgive and repent. Every sermon I listened to ministered to me deeply. Continuing my relationship with Jesus in the secret place was the answer to my recovery.

I want to leave you with hope: there is a light at the end of the tunnel and I am working through it. I am blessed with my amazing family and friends around me. I am not alone. I feel the prayers of others covering my husband and I in this season. I have learnt to see the bigger picture and believe that greater things are to come. I do not know what the future holds but now, more than ever, I am growing in my trust of the Lord. I am fragile and vulnerable, but God is in control.

John 10:10 (AMP)
The thief comes only in order to steal and kill and destroy. I came that they may have *and* enjoy life, and have it in abundance [to the full, till it overflows].

If you can relate to my story, I urge you not to give up the good fight of faith. Keep your heart right and keep your eyes fixed on Jesus. God is making a way out of the wilderness and into a life of abundance. He is in the process of restoring you. Your service to the kingdom has not been forgotten or wasted.

It takes strength, but try to find a way to serve in your church (teas and coffees, nursery, staying behind after church and encouraging someone). Looking outward is what Jesus calls us to do, and in itself will bring healing and purpose, as well as bringing blessing to others.

April 22nd - *Study & Sermon Notes*

Y1 – Ps 32 / Y2 – Ps 136

April 23rd – *No Penalty*

Y1 – Lev 14 & 15 / Y2 – Prov 1 & 2

Romans 8 :1 (NKJV)
There is therefore now *no condemnation* **to those who are in Christ Jesus, who do not walk according to the flesh, but according to the Spirit.**

The word *condemnation* comes from the Greek word meaning 'a sentence' or 'penalty.'[1]

There are many pastor's wives who do not take this text literally or personally, but I want you to know that Paul is speaking to you. One of Satan's devices is to plague your mind with the things of the past, but the responsibility to overcome the 'I can never be forgiven' mindset lies with you.

You must rest in the crystal clear truth that those who are 'in Christ Jesus' are forgiven, there is no sentence hanging over your head nor penalty for the sins of the past. God is not holding a grudge against you!

Romans 8:6 (NKJV)
For to be carnally minded is death, but to be spiritually minded is life and peace.

One of the fruits of being delivered from our sinful past and dwelling in the Spirit is that we can peacefully live life to the fullest. If you have no peace because you've opened a door to the flesh or carnal things of this world, then repentance is what you need. Jesus desires with all of His heart to lift the death sentence from you because you are worth it.

Perhaps you find yourself fighting thoughts of condemnation and are never able to win the battle and get peace. Sometimes we believe what God says about other people, but choose not to believe it for ourselves. Put the thoughts you have against yourself into prison, lock the door and throw the key away. Hating yourself grieves God. He paid the price to set you free because He loves you so much and it is not for you to carry the guilt of your past any longer.

Father, I thank you for provoking my thoughts through this devotion. I have struggled for years with leaving my past behind and accepting that you have forgiven me. Today, I make a commitment to be spiritually minded and walk in the freedom that you purchased for me on the cross. Thank you Jesus, Amen.

April 24th – *Verified Vision*
Y1 – Lev 16 & 17 / Y2 – Prov 3 & 4

Proverbs 29:18 (NIV)
Where there is no revelation, people cast off restraint; but blessed is the one who heeds wisdom's instruction.

Joseph was faithful to the Lord even though his dreams were not realised for many years. God gave him a vision of his life which restrained him from sin and temptation. He fulfilled his dreams, gaining favour throughout, in spite of the adversity he faced.

Growing up, I had a desire to make a difference. I lived in a small, safe village, yet I felt pulled to travel. At age 19, I was the first person saved in a new pioneer church in Australia. I caught the vision for world evangelism instantly. I felt the call to go into the nations and responding to God's prompting, I aligned my life to go. We even got a word that we would go to Zaire.

At 22, I was married, had a baby and a husband, and life was very comfortable! The burden was still heavy on my heart though, but we were a church of 15 people! Then, it happened, after a heart to heart with my husband and a senior pastor who was willing to take the risk, we were sent out to pioneer a church.

Our ministry struggled and we returned to the mother church and all the signs pointed to us sending and not going. Yet, every Thursday night of our fellowship conference, the 'world evangelism' film would be presented and I would weep, trying to shake off the nation's pull on my heart to go. I actually got angry at God, pleading for Him to take away the desire.

Thirty-two years later, we were launched out as pioneer missionaries, as did my daughter and her Congolese (formerly Zaire) husband.

Hold fast to the vision God gives you. Do not grow weary and divert from it and expect God's favour in the sight of others. He causes all things to work for your good as you remain faithful to His purpose for your life.

April 25th – *Sulking Saints*
Y1 – Lev 18 & 19 / Y2 – Prov 5 & 6

1 Kings 21:4 (NKJV)
So Ahab went into his house sullen and displeased because of the word which Naboth the Jezreelite had spoken to him; for he had said, "I will not give you the inheritance of my fathers." And he lay down on his bed, and turned away his face, and would eat no food.

Even though he asked Naboth 'nicely,' King Ahab did not get the vineyard he wanted. It's easy to read this scripture and think, 'Well, that's immature and childish!' He is the king, yet he was lying on his bed sulking. His wife even jumps in to sort out the situation for him, which leads to the murder of Naboth and consequently brings God's judgment upon them both. This is such an extreme sinful reaction, all rooted in emotion which Ahab allowed to dictate his decisions.

I wouldn't imagine many women have this type of response when they 'don't get their way,' but do you sulk at God when things don't work out as you hoped? Do you play the blame game, offer up half-hearted prayer and worship, let words of discontentment and anger fly around in your mind? Even if we think we are hiding our emotions well, inward sulking can result in outward moodiness, being 'quiet,' or sullen.

We should be aware that God will sometimes say, 'No'. Sometimes this 'No' may proceed from the mouths of headship and we must keep a right heart. We might have even specifically prayed and believed, but in God's infinite wisdom He knows what is best for us. When things don't go how we wanted, outlined, or expected, we must rest in the knowledge that God has a perfect plan. Sometimes we aren't going to understand it all until a lot further down the line, maybe not even until we reach eternity, but we must trust in His goodness.

Romans 11:33 (NKJV)
Oh, the depth of the riches both of the wisdom and knowledge of God! How unsearchable are His judgments and His ways past finding out!

April 26th – *Upper Hand*

Y1 – Lev 20 & 21 / Y2 – Prov 7 & 8

Deuteronomy 28:13 (NIV)
The LORD will make you the head, not the tail. If you pay attention to the commands of the LORD your God that I give you this day and carefully follow them, you will always be at the top, never at the bottom.

Have you ever met someone who has authority, makes clear decisions, strongly, but fairly gives a command, and is in control?

When I did, it was this part of her character that captivated me. She spoke with dominion and I wanted that, but how? So, I asked her what I could do to obtain it. She humbly responded by saying that she fully believed in the Word of God and His promises. No negotiation, no doubt, and she gave no time to listen to the lies of the enemy. She depended on the Word, wholly trusted that God heard her prayers, and believed that God can and will move in people's lives.

Our scripture reveals that the necessary condition for gaining dominion is to 'pay attention to the commands of the Lord' and 'follow them.'

Are you struggling to have control in certain situations? Ask yourself if you are truly listening and doing what God has asked of you?

My friend, who is also a pastor's wife, believes and obeys the commands of Jesus, so it is no coincidence that she lives life at the 'top' as a Christian. She says things like, 'If Jesus is my Saviour, then Jesus really *is* my Saviour,' and, 'If we are to treat others as we would like to be treated, then so be it, no questions asked.' She takes her words seriously and has a clear confidence in Jesus, which empowers people around her to do the same.

Every Christian who follows and obeys can have the upper hand, be the head and not the tail, and rise above to conquer. Do not give Satan access to your mind, but allow the Word of God to strengthen your character so that you may walk in authority and dominion.

April 27th – *Historical Women*

Y1 – Lev 22 & 23 / Y2 – Prov 9 & 10

Corrie Ten Boom (1892-1983)

Corrie was born and raised in the Netherlands, her family were Christians and members of the Dutch Reformed Church. The family's faith meant that they kept a deep respect for the Jewish people even as World War II began and the Nazi regime grew stronger. Her father owned a watch shop with an upstairs apartment in which they lived and it became a refuge and hiding place for those hunted by the Nazis. They would have 5 to 6 people hiding with them, for hours or days, before moving to another safe house. It was the family's way of showing their Christian love and it is estimated they were instrumental in saving about 800 lives.[1]

In February 1944, the Ten Booms were betrayed, their house raided, and the family was arrested. Miraculously, the six people hiding at the time were not found and were later taken to other safe houses. Corrie's family was held in prison initially, where her father died after only ten days, and she and her sister Betsie were sent to the Ravensbrück Concentration Camp. Life was very difficult there, yet the sisters would hold worship services, read from a Bible they had smuggled in, and shared the love of Jesus with others.[2]

Sadly, Betsie died in December of 1944. Just days later, Corrie was released and made her way back to the Netherlands, where she set up a rehabilitation centre for concentration camp survivors. Corrie started traveling the world as a public speaker and wrote several books including 'The Hiding Place'.[3]

In 1947, Corrie was in Germany giving a talk about forgiveness when she came face-to-face with a former guard. He told her how he had repented and became a Christian and then asked her for forgiveness, stretching out his hand. Corrie knew she had to forgive him, 'I stood there with the coldness clutching my heart... but forgiveness is an act of the will, and the will can function regardless of the temperature of the heart. And so woodenly, mechanically, I thrust my hand into the one stretched out to me. And as I did, an incredible thing took place. The current started in my shoulder, raced down my arm, sprang into our joined hands. And then this healing warmth seemed to flood my whole being, bringing tears to my eyes ... I had never known God's love so intensely as I did then.'[4]

April 28th - *Testimony*

Y1 – Ps 33 / Y2 – Ps 137

Healing Vessel by Charlotte

What a busy Sunday! Cooking for the new converts and fellowshipping was a lot of fun, but I had been functioning all day with a very painful shoulder. As I walked into church on Sunday night with my three children, one of the ladies noticed the pain in my face. I was struggling to lift my youngest child and she asked if I was okay. 'Yes, I'm fine, thank you,' I responded, 'I just have a bad shoulder.' I demonstrated that I couldn't move it in any direction and before I knew it, she had laid her hands on me and was praying for my deliverance.

For a few seconds I wasn't even aware what she was doing, she was so quick, but astonishingly I knew immediately I could feel a difference. I started to move my arm around in 360-degree circles. I was healed and the pain has never returned. God used this precious lady in my church to bring healing me.

Two things struck me right away. Firstly, I felt challenged to do the same for others, to step out in faith and believe God for healing as she did because faith without works is dead, right?

Secondly, I realised that God provided the vessel for my healing inside my own church. My, how we can underestimate the faith, abilities and gifting of men and women in *our own* congregations. God forbid the day that we compare, complain, put restrictions on, and criticise the people God has already given us.

1 Corinthians 1:27 (NIV)
But God chose the foolish things of the world to shame the wise; God chose the weak things of the world to shame the strong

Whilst the world may think this lovely lady foolish or her prayer foolish, God used her powerfully that day. Sometimes we can expect so little from people, but there is potential in every soul who attends our churches and God can help us to always see His purpose at work in them.

April 29th - *Study & Sermon Notes*

Y1 – Ps 34 / Y2 – Ps 138

April 30th – *Church Rebels*
Y1 – Lev 24 & 25 / Y2 – Prov 11 & 12

At any stage in church development, people can begin to speak negative words that gain momentum and sometimes this can lead to full rebellion against both our husbands and the church. This can be such a testing time, as previously we have loved and cared for these people.

How do we react to rebels?

I have found through the years of our ministry that some people just aren't willing to follow the biblical procedure of reconciliation. It was especially heart-breaking when some long-standing members of our church with unfounded issues chose to vent against my husband rather than come to him to get clarity and work it out. I was saddened because I knew from experience that it would inevitably cause them to leave the church.

I chose as a wife not to listen, but to keep a good relationship with headship and carry on serving the church wholeheartedly, even with those involved. I kept my head down and let God work it through believing the old truth, 'Right comes out right!' It is God's battle in the heavenlies and not my own.

Ephesians 6:12 (NKJV)
"For we do not wrestle against flesh and blood, but against principalities…".

I continued to pray for the people involved, their salvation, marriages, families, and that their lives wouldn't be destroyed by the very words they were speaking. I also prayed God would help me maintain a good attitude. Eventually, they left the church and missed out on the full purposes of God in their lives.

Throughout this time, I encouraged the ladies of the church and remained strong for my husband. It was a stressful time, but I knew God would work it through. It is important to prepare ourselves in prayer and through His Word, as testing seasons will come.

Lord Jesus, our church is dealing with and suffering the pain of a church split, unrighteous words spoken and allegations. People are confused and hurting. I am asking you to protect my husband, children and congregation. Help them to discern what is right in this circumstance and encourage them through the preaching of the Word. Fight for us. Amen.

May 1st – *Jehovah Nissi*
Y1 – Lev 26 & 27 / Y2 – Prov 13 & 14

Exodus 17:15 (NKJV)
And Moses built an altar and called it The Lord is my Banner (Jehovah-Nissi).

Of the different names of God, this one confused me for years. As a child, I learned about it in Sunday school, but could never grasp how or why God could literally turn into a flag (a banner). Well, you'll be pleased to know that I've come quite a long way in my comprehension and coupled with this, my hair is no longer blonde (sadly).

For the sake of context and insight, the reason that Moses built an altar is because the Israelites had won a long, hard battle against a formidable tribe called the Amalekites, which took some major team effort. They had been traveling through the desert and were suddenly ambushed. Moses went to the top of a hill to oversee the battle, and held out his staff (the same one that he used to do miracles in Egypt and to part the Red Sea).

Exodus 17:11-13 (NKJV)
And so it was, when Moses held up his hand, that Israel prevailed; and when he let down his hand, Amalek prevailed. But Moses' hands *became* heavy; so they took a stone and put *it* under him, and he sat on it. And Aaron and Hur supported his hands, one on one side, and the other on the other side; and his hands were steady... So Joshua defeated Amalek and his people with the edge of the sword.

Miraculously, the Lord intervened and the Israelites prevailed as long as Moses lifted up the rod. When he became tired, they jumped right in and held up his arms, just like a banner. 'The lesson is quite clear. The rod was a symbol and pledge of God's presence and power. Lowered it could not be seen. It was as though God was not there and therefore not in the mind of the people.'[1]

Do you keep God visible, lifted up, and in the front of your mind like a banner in the midst of your battles?

With God, we can overcome anything.

May 2nd – *Say What!*

Y1 – Zeph 1 & 2 / Y2 – Prov 15 & 16

Proverbs 12:22 (NIV)
The LORD detests lying lips, but He delights in people who are trustworthy.

A couple of years into pioneering, I began to ask God to give weight to my words. Jesus said to Simon, "Follow me," and guess what? He did. I desired that gift so people would come to know Jesus through my words. I laughed to myself when I thought how the knock-on effect would be my children leaping into obedience at the immense authority of my words!

As I began contending for this dimension in my life, God surprised me with a different and unexpected revelation. He asked me 'Is exaggeration a form of lying?' Got me right there! I am a little bit of an actress, loud, bubbly, love to tell stories, make people laugh, and often an exaggerator; but did that mean I was a liar? Was it possible that my habit of exaggeration nullified the weight of my words?

I began to think about my conduct and observe conversations around me. I noticed that typically, emotions and feelings dominate discussions between women and I would use exaggeration to be humorous. Statements like, 'I could eat a horse' or 'my husband is going to kill me' lighten a conversation, but we must be careful of phrases like, 'she hates me' because those words are capable of manipulating the other person's opinion. It's scary how we as humans can so easily embellish the language to suit how we feel, and what we've said isn't actually true.

God challenged me and I realised the error of my ways. Instead of using exaggeration like 'they never…' (which is a lie) I began saying 'they rarely' (which is the truth). I understand now that explosive language can be a cover up for insecurity.

Few people may relate to my concern about exaggeration, but the general message here is to consider your words. Make sure that only truth proceeds from your lips, not deception, exaggeration, lies or manipulation. An honest and trustworthy person who walks in humility brings security and peace to the people around them and glorifies the King.

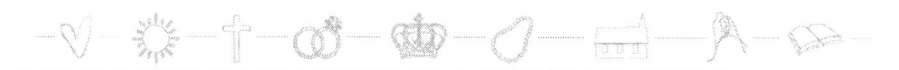

May 3rd – *Avoiding Contention*
Y1 – Zeph 3 / Y2 – Prov 17 & 18

Proverbs 21:19 (NKJV)
Better to dwell in the wilderness, Than with a contentious and angry woman.

Proverbs 27:15 (NKJV)
A continual dripping on a very rainy day and a contentious woman are alike.

Contentious is defined as causing or likely to cause an argument.[1] The picture of constant dripping rain is a woman who annoys those around her with non-stop arguing, questioning and nagging.

Proverbs 15:18 (AMP)
A hot-tempered man stirs up strife, but he who is slow to anger *and* patient calms disputes.

Proverbs 14:29 (NKJV)
He who is **slow to wrath has great understanding, but** *he who is* **impulsive exalts folly.**

On a daily basis, there are many opportunities for us to be contentious and stir up anger in conversation with our husbands, children, friends and with people in our congregation. Of course, there are times we do need to speak up, but these scriptures show we should be thoughtful and consider what we say. By being slow to anger, we allow God to help us avoid damaging situations and be an example to others. Marriages, relationships and churches can be destroyed by words spoken in anger and haste, with no consideration of the other person.

Have you heard the joke, "What's the difference between a battery and my wife? The battery has a positive side!'

The truth is, she may feel like she has a good reason, but the argumentative wife is unrighteous, unbearable and a bad example. Her negative charge affects the whole household and can be quite tangible to those in her company. The hope is that with God's help she can change. No situation is unworkable.

May 4th – *Football Trivia*

Y1 – Hag 1 & 2 / Y2 – Prov 19 & 20

1 Corinthians 9:22 (MSG)
I kept my bearings in Christ—but I entered their world and tried to experience things from their point of view. I've become just about every sort of servant there is in my attempts to lead those I meet into a God-saved life. I did all this because of the Message. I didn't just want to talk about it; I wanted to be in on it!

My husband has never been that interested in football. A couple of years ago, he realised that it was limiting his effectiveness in working with men in church because as soon as the conversation about football came up he was unable to participate.

Purely from his desire to reach men, my husband set out to learn all things football and soon became quite the expert! When I listened to him talk to new converts about the sport, I was seriously impressed; he'd gone out of his comfort zone, and it worked! I felt inspired to do the same, so when God laid upon my heart to reach out to a deaf lady in our congregation. I began to learn some basic sign language and asked her if she'd be willing to teach me some more. Whilst it was a slow process (because I have the memory of a fish!), we gradually built up a friendship and I was able to minister to her.

Paul's example teaches us how to be the most effective soul winner there is. It means broadening our knowledge and skill set beyond our natural leanings by being *genuinely* interested in the interests of others. It may mean meeting a lady for a walk (or dare I say a run) even though you hate exercise, or getting your nails done even though you'd never consider it by yourself. Paul entered their world and God used it for His glory. If you are willing to experience things from their point of view, God will help you and give you the joy of winning people to Him.

Father God, I thank you for the people you have given me to love, invest in and take care of. I ask you to equip me uniquely and continually with knowledge and wisdom in serving them, many of whom I struggle to relate to. Give me compassion, understanding and patience. Just like Paul, I don't desire only to talk about the Word but to be a part of it. Thank you Jesus for all that You can and will do through me. Amen.

May 5th – *Testimony*

Y1 – Ps 35 / Y2 – Ps 139

Salvation Story by Cheryl

I was born in Jamaica, the third child of five children. I would say my life started out riddled with struggles and disruptions as my mother ran from one abusive relationship to the next. I was called 'a child of circumstance' because my father was already married with four children when my mother had me. Not long after my birth, my father had a mental breakdown, so I never knew him.

By age seven, due to being exposed to domestic violence and abuse, I became withdrawn and emotionally detached. All I knew to do was to survive, having to grow up before my time. By the age of twelve, my mother was on her fourth relationship, a holiday romance that led to marriage, and I was separated from my other siblings because my mum and I moved to England. We moved into my new stepbrother's house, living in cramped conditions, and my mother got pregnant right away. It wasn't long before the abuse began. We were in a foreign country with no support.

I felt like the world was against me and nowhere was safe. I was teased at school because of my accent, my body was changing and my hair was falling out. I hated men because they were the cause of my woes, and I sure did not identify with girls because they were weak and stupid. The only way I knew how to protect myself was to build a wall of anger around me. I would get in fights at school and be disrespectful to the teachers. As a last resort, I was assigned a school psychologist. This was actually a turning point in my life. Jenny, a Baptist minister's wife, was the most loving 'New Zealander' I had ever met. She was patient with me, talked me through my experiences, and helped me to navigate and adapt to living in a new country with new academic and social demands. She invited me into her home and showed me a different perspective on life. Most evenings after school were spent at her house and I would go home just in time for bed.

At the age of 13, Jenny took me to a Billy Graham crusade where I gave my life to Jesus. I attended her church, but it consisted of much older people, so to balance things out I started going to a youth group near my home. There I met a friend who got filled with the Holy Ghost, but speaking in tongues was discouraged at her church. Then one Saturday, we met some young people who were on an outreach and they invited us to a revival at their church. We decided to attend and it felt like I got saved all over again. God began to strip away the shame and guilt and, even though it was uncomfortable, this is when the change really began in my life.

The journey has not always been easy, but it has been worth it. When I was just 22, my mother had a mental breakdown and I had to take on the responsibility of caring for my two younger brothers. I experienced mental assaults and anxiety because of the pressure and coming to terms with her sickness. However, in those dark times, I learnt to pray in the midnight hours and take dominion over my mind and thoughts. Two scriptures that sustained me:

Psalms 56:3 (ESV)
When I am afraid, I put my trust in you.

Timothy 1:7 (NKJV)
For God has not given us a spirit of fear, but of power and of love and of a sound mind.

My husband and I have now been married 26 years with 22 years in the ministry. I rejoice today because the curse of dysfunction has been broken in my family and I have been set free. Thank you, Jesus!

May 6th – *Study & Sermon Notes*

Y1 – Ps 36 / Y2 – Ps 140

May 7th - *Forgive ... Repeat!*

Y1 – Rom 1 & 2 / Y2 – Prov 21 & 22

Luke 17:3-4 (NIV)
So watch yourselves. "If your brother or sister sins against you, rebuke them; and if they repent, forgive them. Even if they sin against you seven times in a day and seven times come back to you saying, 'I repent,' you must forgive them."

The epitome of forgiveness is Jesus sacrificing himself on the cross for our sins, so we could be forgiven by our Father in heaven. This is a reference point and a reminder that no matter how a person has sinned against us, we have to find it within ourselves to forgive, because nothing compares to the forgiveness that we have been given when we abide in Christ.

There are numerous scriptures on forgiveness, but this one is full of detail. It directly instructs us on how to respond when a brother or sister in Christ sins against us. Some would argue that it is easier to forgive a 'sinner' because 'they know not what they do' so we tend to let them off the hook. However, this scripture tells us that we as Christians are also going to miss the mark at some point and will find ourselves in need of forgiveness.

Jesus commands us to forgive. How can we expect the Lord to forgive us if we don't have the heart to forgive others?[1] Remember the parable of the servant in the Bible who refused to forgive an insignificant debt against him, when prior to this offence he had been forgiven of an enormous debt?[2] He was cast away because unforgiveness is a deal breaker for God.

Is there someone you need to forgive? Do you repeatedly have issues with unforgiveness?

To let go isn't easy, but it is an uncomplicated act. Look to the Cross for the example that we need to forgive and let it encourage you. Trust God to heal your wounds! Begin the process with a prayer of forgiveness and allow Jesus to take over. You *can* do this!

May 8th – *Hold Up!*

Y1 – Rom 3 & 4 / Y2 – Prov 23 & 24

Joshua 3:1-3 (NLT)
Early the next morning Joshua and all the Israelites left Acacia Grove and arrived at the banks of the Jordan River, where they camped before crossing. Three days later the Israelite officers went through the camp, giving these instructions to the people: "When you see the Levitical priests carrying the Ark of the Covenant of the Lord your God, move out from your positions and follow them."

Joshua had become the leader of Israel after the death of Moses. God gave him the wonderful promise that they were going to have victory in the promised land. They were so close, yet God told them to wait and rest for three days before implementing the plan.

In the ministry, we know the vision we are aiming towards, but we might feel we're in a place of waiting like Joshua. He had to wait for the ark of the covenant (God's presence) to guide them. God has a plan for our victory, and although this may be difficult, it may also involve a time of waiting.

What are you waiting for? Do you trust that God can meet your needs or wants? Or have you taken matters into your own hands?

It's important to note that during this time of waiting the people were not idle, for Joshua had told them to consecrate themselves. When you are in a period of waiting and it seems that nothing is happening, consecrate yourself to prepare for God to move. Establish yourself into a routine of prayer, praise, Bible reading, and cast away anything that makes you unholy.

Lord, it is hard to be in a period of waiting. Help us see these times of rest and waiting as necessary for the victory and let us use them to focus on being set apart and holy so when the battle comes we'll be ready. Amen.

May 9th – *Speculate to Accumulate*

Y1 – Rom 5 & 6 / Y2 – Prov 25 & 26

Ezekiel 37:4-6 (MSG)
He said to me, "Prophesy over these bones: 'Dry bones, listen to the Message of God!'" God, the Master, told the dry bones, "Watch this: I'm bringing the breath of life to you and you'll come to life. I'll attach sinews to you, put meat on your bones, cover you with skin, and breathe life into you. You'll come alive and you'll realize that I am God!"

When my husband and I took over the pastorate of our church, we specifically prayed for men, money, and a miracle building (I'm sure you might have the same needs). In other words, we were speculating. This means that in order for you to see something *happen*, you have to be able to see something *happening*. You must be able to see it with the eyes of faith and believe God for what isn't currently there! We contended for the supernatural, knowing that building a church wasn't a work of man, but a work of God.

Ezekiel looked at the dry bones and God posed the question, 'Can these dry bones live?' *Did Ezekiel speculate?* It doesn't sound like it. He responded, 'You know Lord,' which is a spiritual-sounding version of, 'I'm not saying no, but I'm not saying yes either!'

Sometimes we respond to God as Ezekiel did. We look around at our church and all we can see are dry bones. No life at all, but with God those dry bones can live again! *Can you see it by faith?* I heard a pastor once say, 'Always keep an eye out for the little miracles, as this is what keeps the ship sailing.'

Lord, I thank you for every precious person you have brought into this church. I ask that you would stretch my faith so that I can see the potential for all that you have planned for this congregation. I believe that dry bones can live and ask that your resurrection power would be at work. Amen.

May 10th – *Kingdom Hierarchy*

Y1 – Rom 7 & 8 / Y2 – Prov 27 & 28

Galatians 3:28 (NKJV)
There is neither Jew nor Greek, there is neither slave nor free, there is neither male nor female; for you are all one in Christ Jesus.

Paul is speaking to the Galatians who were under the impression that there is a kingdom hierarchy between the Jews and the Gentiles. Paul explains that in Christ we are all equal and united. There is no culture, race or gender that is higher-ranking in Christianity. Whether you have been saved three years or thirty, God doesn't prefer an older saint to a younger. We are all valuable to Jesus.

It may sound far-fetched, but some believe that the pastor's wife is somehow superior to the members of her congregation. We must be careful not to fall into this trap of spiritual pride. I have a friend who has been called Pastor by members of her church and she has been quick to kindly correct them. She lets them know that her husband is the pastor, she is their friend. We have different roles, but one is not above the other. God had given us particular job to do and it is our duty to fulfil it.

We are each running our own Christian race, learning as we go, through prayer and guidance from other Godly women. Let's encourage each other in our faith. No one is more highly esteemed in God's eyes than another, but we are all one in Christ Jesus.

Galatians 2:6 (NLT)
And the leaders of the church had nothing to add to what I was preaching. (By the way, their reputation as great leaders made no difference to me, for God has no favourites.)

May 11th – *Pioneering Toddlers*

Y1 – Rom 9 & 10 / Y2 – Prov 29 & 30

Psalms 27: 14 (NKJV)
Wait on the Lord; Be of good courage, And He shall strengthen your heart; Wait, I say, on the LORD!

Few can appreciate the pressures and strains upon a pastor's wife. A pioneer work with no Sunday school or nursery provision, not being able to give yourself to worship or listening to the preaching of the Word while you are keeping your own small children still-ish, let alone supporting other members.

How many sisters will relate to my experience of my two year old walking to the back of church to her pram, and sitting on her potty to have a wee before I even noticed she had moved! Or carrying out two small children in the middle of service, one of whom was hollering at the top of her lungs! For months I wasn't able to hear my husband's carefully prepared sermons, words that could have encouraged, loved and challenged me. I found myself irritated with the children, pressured by others present and desperate to be spiritually fed, my emotions would boil over. Dear Sister, I *know* I am not alone.

With little growth over a two year period it did indeed feel like we were just pioneering, establishing and discipling tiny children, who had no clue. When I look back its actually very funny, at the time it was the greatest distress to me, but our scripture says it all: Wait on Jesus, be of good courage. The Lord promises to strengthen your heart if you would simply stop, stay and hang around Him.

Hanging with God every day (I like that), in my morning devotional time, has completely changed my frustrated perspective. I am more inspired and listen to more sermons in the week while doing the household chores or on my way to work. I have learnt to be patient.

Just remember that the beautiful children God has entrusted us to raise, are just children, not emotionally controlled adults. We expect good behaviour but be reasonable and sensitive. It is all too easy to lose your rag but it only takes a moment to establish how a situation needs to be dealt with. Take a few seconds to calm yourself, assess underlying issues and make a judgement call. Don't bite to soon, the congregation will understand a bit of noise (or they will learn), God will help you as He did me.

May 12th – *Testimony*

Y1 – Ps 37 / Y2 – Ps 141

Angels Encamp by Jacqui

It had been a long, but refreshing week. We had driven overnight from London in time to have church on Sunday morning at home in Scotland. After service, I drove over an hour to have lunch with my parents and collect the children, the words of my husband still in my ear, 'Make sure you are home in time for Sunday evening service.' I waved goodbye to my parents, then sped down the dual-carriageway, passing the one solitary car on the road. The children were asleep in the cozy car, the sun glistened on the freezing North Sea, and the worship music soothed my soul.

Bang! I held tightly onto the steering wheel and put my foot on the brakes. The central reservation flashed before me. Bang! I saw the car I just passed heading towards me. Bang! The next thing I knew my car was stopped, facing the correct way on the side of the road as if I had just pulled over and parked. Immediately, I looked in the back seat to check on the kids, they were still asleep. 'Oh no,' I thought, 'I'm going to be late for church!' As I got out of the car I was approached by a very visibly shocked man who looked as if he had just seen a ghost. I asked him, 'Are you alright?' He just stared at my bulging tummy (I was seven months pregnant) and replied, 'I can't believe you're alive!'

Looking over the damage to the car, he proceeded to tell me what he saw: As I had sped past him, he observed that I was over the speed limit. An instant later he saw a flurry of dust from the kerb and my car heading towards the central reservation. It hit the barrier on the passenger side, spun halfway around and flipped up on two wheels, then one wheel, then hovered a moment before the rear side hit the barrier. This caused the car to turn back around to face the way it had been travelling, pass over the two lanes and come to a stop on the side of the road. He could not understand why the car's speed and force had not sent the car tumbling. He was shaking. I was praising God.

Angels, I knew it, angels were encamped around that car holding it up. There is no logical explanation because the laws of motion and gravity should have flipped the car.

Psalm 91:11-12 (KJV)
For he gives angels charge over thee, to keep thee in all thy ways. They shall bear thee up in their hands...

The car was written off. The report stated that I had hit the side of the kerb at considerable speed, forcing the car to collide with the central reservation and twisting the whole chassis. A second of shutting my eyes was all it took. People often think they have time to accept Jesus before they die, but I know we are just a blink away from eternity.

1 Corinthians 15:52 (NKJV)
In a moment, in the twinkling of an eye, ... and we shall be changed.

May 13th – *Study & Sermon Notes*

Y1 – Ps 38 / Y2 – Ps 142

May 14th – *Tight Grip*
Y1 – Rom 11 & 12 / Y2 – Prov 31

Hebrews 2:1-3 (NKJV)
Therefore we must give the more earnest heed to the things we have heard, lest we drift away. For if the word spoken through angels proved steadfast, and every transgression and disobedience received a just reward, how shall we escape if we neglect so great a salvation, which at the first began to be spoken by the Lord, and was confirmed to us by those who heard Him

Hebrews 2:1 (MSG)
It's crucial that we keep a firm grip on what we've heard so that we don't drift off.

This passage speaks very clearly about keeping a firm grip, lest we drift away from serving the Lord. To drift is to move slowly away from our course,[1] so slowly in fact that it might not be noticeable, and is completely unintentional. Just as a child tightly holds a piece of chocolate, so must we keep a firm and unyielding grip on our relationship with Jesus.

Additionally, we must hang on to, remember, and act upon all that we have heard and received through preaching, reading the Bible, and God's personal words to us.

Lastly, the scripture speaks about neglecting our great salvation. When we neglect, fail to care for properly[2], or nurture our relationship with God, we are starving our spirit. We need to prioritise our devotional life because it is vital in the fight against drifting. As a mother at home with children, I have found that there is no structured time for prayer unless I make it and no one to be accountable to unless I'm intentional. We must build strong habits that allow us time with God and in His Word to refresh us daily.

Lord, thank you for my salvation and your steadfast Word. Help me to stay firm through the ups and downs of life, so that I may not drift. Help me to prioritise your Word, so that you would speak to me through it. Let me in turn be an unwavering light for others. Amen.

May 15th – *Chicken Lover*

Y1 – Rom 13 & 14 / Y2 – Ecc 1 & 2

Philippians 2:3-4 (NKJV)
***Let* nothing *be done* through selfish ambition or conceit, but in lowliness of mind let each esteem others better than himself. Let each of you look out not only for his own interests, but also for the interests of others.**

A family came to a fellowship at my house with *stacks* of Caribbean style jerk chicken. Oh my days, it was so yummy! I could have eaten that BBQ gravy with rice and peas all day long. When it came time for people to leave, there was still lots of chicken left. The family had said to us that they wanted to bless us with the food. My eyes were as big as golf balls. 'Oh yes, no cooking tomorrow for me, dinner is already prepared!' But almost as soon as my heart started to rejoice, it stopped. Several voices perked up, volunteering to take some home. I was very irritated by this, as this chicken was for *me*, surely my family deserved it!

Proverbs 19:17 (NKJV)
He who has pity on the poor lends to the Lord, And He will pay back what he has given.

Oh, how hard it was to sacrifice that chicken! However, it didn't belong to me, it belonged to the Lord as an offering and who am I to take that from others? Who knows how much it cost that family for that meal in money, time and love to get the perfect balance of spice and sweetness? They sacrificed in order to bless others.

God sees when we sacrifice and He wants us to put others above our own needs. I didn't need that chicken; I mean I really *wanted* it, but I didn't *need* it. The other people that asked for it, a recovering drug abuser and a young student, had a much greater need than mine.

Big or small, a sacrifice is a sacrifice, and the Lord knew I really wanted that chicken. Always remember that He sees when we give to others (Hebrews 6:10).

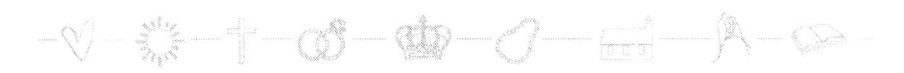

May 16th – *Effective Love*
Y1 – Rom 15 & 16 / Y2 – Ecc 3 & 4

1 John 3:1 (NKJV)
Behold what manner of love that the Father has bestowed on us, that we should be called children of God!...

1 John 3:18 (MSG)
My dear children let's not just talk about love; let's practice real love. This is the only way we'll know that we're living truly, living in God's reality. It's also the way to *shut down* debilitating self-criticism, even when there's something to it ...

1 John 3:21 (NKJV)
Beloved if our heart does not condemn us, we have confidence toward God.

If you condemn yourself, it hinders your confidence in God and therefore hinders your ability to love! Just like water is wet, God is love! His love must translate into your own life!

1 John 3:11, 14, 16 (NKJV)
... You heard from the beginning, that we should love one another... We know that we have passed from death to life, because we love the brethren. He who does love his brother abides in death ... By this we know love, because He laid down His life for us. And we also ought to lay down our lives for the brethren.

I ask you with all sincerity, please stop criticising yourself, lest you end up in a spiritual wheelchair, crippled by your own thoughts and potentially made ineffective in the kingdom of God. Have you ever heard your own child or loved one speak poorly of themselves? It's awful and enough to cause us a heartbreak. That is how God feels when our self-talk is negative. If you have the assurance of God's love for you, then it flows through you and changes lives.

Lord Jesus, You are love. I love you and I am desperate for You to help me. Show me how to walk in that love, and how to stop accepting the lies of the enemy. I am making a commitment, from this day forward, I renounce my self-hatred and will cast my burdens on you! Thank You Jesus for this deliverance! Amen.

May 17th – *Subtle Sin*

Y1 – Num 1 & 2 / Y2 – Ecc 5 & 6

Ezekiel 16 :49 (ESV)
Behold, this was the guilt of your sister Sodom: she and her daughters had pride, excess of food, and prosperous ease, but did not aid the poor and needy.

The people of Sodom had such abundance that it gave them a sense of security to the point that they felt no need. However, they abused this blessing through overindulgence, became prideful and insensitive to those in need, and more worryingly, unmoved by the potential judgment of God. We also live in a world of abundance and over indulgence. Never has the world had so much food, and yet so much starvation and poverty exists. It is a stark warning Ezekiel gives us of the people of Sodom.

Proverbs 23:21 (NIV)
For drunkards and gluttons become poor, and drowsiness clothes them in rags.

One commentary on this verse says, '... and drowsiness shall clothe a man with rags; excessive eating and drinking brings drowsiness on men, unfits them for business, and makes them idle and slothful; and spending all on their bellies, they have nothing for their backs, and are clothed in rags.' When there is abundance, you can develop a mindset of squandering, especially with food.
Why restrain yourself when there is so much choice and delicious food? To squander food through waste or unhealthy choices is not what God delights in. Gluttony is a sin, plain and clear. In the Old Testament, over indulging was in-part a reason parents could take their child to the elders to be judged (Deuteronomy 21:20). We thank God that's not the case now or Boxing Day would be a tense time.

Take some time to consider your relationship with food. Do you eat when you are not hungry? Do you grab snacks on the go because you haven't made the time to prepare? Are you constantly dieting? Do you feel hopeless? Do not despair, God can and will help you.

God help me see where I am overindulging with food. Help me identify why I am dependent on this. Thank You for Your grace and mercy that can help me overcome this through the power of Jesus Christ. Amen.

May 18th – *Soul Rest*

Y1 – Num 3 & 4 / Y2 – Ecc 7 & 8

Matthew 11:28-30 (NKJV)
Come to Me, all you who labour and are heavy laden, and I will give you rest. Take My yoke upon you and learn from Me, for I am gentle and lowly in heart, and you will find rest for your souls. For My yoke is easy and My burden is light.

Isn't it just amazing when a scripture is brought alive in your own life. You have called on the Lord and He has met with you.

My new job took me right out of my comfort zone (again), and boy do I like my comfort zone. "They made the wrong decision. This is beyond my abilities. I'm can't absorb everything asked of me. I am out of my depth. I have to run away."

Now, I know my Saviour, my Lord, and He knows my name. There is nothing more precious than sitting down and talking with Him.

It is in the coming to Him that a way can be found. It is in the sitting with Him comes the quietening of my soul. Labouring and being heavy laden are all parts of a normal and successful life!

Oxen are used to plough fields. With a wooden "harness" across their shoulders, they pull *together*. In Jesus' presence I latch myself up to Him. "Lord I need your help. This is beyond me. How do I get through this? Do you have any ideas?"

I learn from Him as my thoughts settle and ideas come to me. I have to talk to someone. I had to find the courage to explain my thoughts, my fears and express the problems I was seeing. My manager spoke wisdom. Work out the priority for the moment. Complete the task. Work out the next priority. Complete the task. Don't focus on the stuff building up around you.

In prayer I deliberately and mentally latched Jesus' yoke to me, reigned in my thoughts, and learned the ropes. *We* pulled *together*.

I have found rest for my soul. Sweet! I am in a job I love and find satisfying, and I pray God will be glorified in and through my life.

How precious it is when the Word of God becomes *my* Word of God. He is *my* Lord, *my* Saviour, *my* Redeemer.

May 19th – *Testimony*

Y1 – Ps 39 / Y2 – Ps 143

Green-Eyed Monster by Anon

Proverbs 14:30 (NIV)
A heart at peace gives life to the body, but envy rots the bones.

My husband grew up in church, was moral, spiritual, generous, and had adopted Godly qualities in his life. I, on the other hand didn't have a Christian upbringing, was lost in sin, and struggled to focus on anything other than myself. I gave my life to Christ when I was seventeen, so when I married at eighteen years old, I was a relatively new convert and God was still peeling back the layers of immorality. I desperately wanted to believe that I was pure and my life had been cleansed by the blood of Jesus, but when I looked at my husband I felt like filth. He had saved himself for marriage, whilst I gave myself to sexual immorality at the age of thirteen years. In my eyes, he was a 10 out of 10 and I had hit the jackpot! This heightened my feelings of inadequacy and propelled my manic jealousy.

My first Bible conference as a married woman should have been a joyous and God-centred event, but I quickly became consumed with how many 'more beautiful' women there were around me. Did they want my husband? After this realisation of my own character, several emotions hit the surface and my excitement was lost. Did I trust my husband? Of course, he was a man with great integrity! However, my mind was telling me that other women were like snakes with an agenda. Jealousy was eating me alive, but I kept these feelings inside for fear of my husband thinking less of me. Insecurity led me to act like I had everything together so he wouldn't see how worthless I felt. I even allowed friends and family to become the opposition. Whilst I refused to admit these things, my actions demonstrated I was tense about something.

I cannot remember the exact moment of change, but things came to a point where I had to confess to both Jesus and my husband. Through lots of prayer, repeatedly casting out demonic strategies, and renewing my mind through the Word, I was set free. I had to apologise to several people and let go of the crazy things I genuinely believed about others. God helped me to see that my sin had been washed completely clean at the Cross. I was made new when Jesus saved me, I was no less of a Christian because of my past, and I am a testimony to God's glory and the power of salvation! Praise God!

The persistent jealousy eased and I found I could allow myself to build friendships once more. God gradually restored my perspective and helped me focus on the future and strive for a better path. My marriage is happy and secure because I have learnt to see myself as Christ sees me. I can control my thoughts, choose what I allow to take a foothold in my heart, and let Jesus reign over my life.

May 20th – *Study & Sermon Notes*

Y1 – Ps 40 / Y2 – Ps 144

May 21st – *Softly Spoken*

Y1 – Num 5 & 6 / Y2 – Ecc 9 & 10

Proverbs 15:1 (NKJV)
A soft answer turns away wrath, but a harsh word stirs up anger.

This is a very familiar and often used verse of scripture, but God really spoke to me and gave me a fresh revelation. This area of anger has been something my husband and I have both had to deal with. It may not seem like it to those around me, but I can be a bit of a hot head! For a long time I never saw myself as an angry person; but when I looked deeper I found I was. I often found myself getting mad and annoyed at small things.

A piece of advice my pastor and his wife gave me before we went out to pioneer was that I *can* chill and relax, and things *can* be calm. I often remind myself of this when dealing with people and our church. Not everything goes my way, but that is *ok*! I am learning to speak with soft words, and let the preaching be what ministers to people. I started to look at this scripture from a different perspective. When someone speaks to me with harsh or cruel words, I am more likely to respond in anger, but if they speak to me softly and with kindness, I naturally return the same tone. I hope I can be that soft, kind person when speaking to others.

Are you quick tempered? Do you speak harshly when you are frustrated with someone?

I don't think this applies to every woman; I would have looked past this before, thought it irrelevant and said this isn't for me. Until, however, I looked deeper and challenged my thinking. As the saying goes, 'the more people, the more problems' and I might add 'the more you need to speak soft words'.

Pray that God would identify and reveal anger or the tendency towards harsh words within yourself. Pray for wisdom in these situations; that He would show you the soft answer you can give.

May 22nd – *Heart Tests*

Y1 – Num 7 & 8 / Y2 – Ecc 11 & 12

Colossians 3:2 (NKJV)
Set your mind on things above, not on things on the earth.

Before becoming a Christian, I would travel to an area and then move on after so many months. I experienced rich and poor people's lives, and realised that everyone has the same stresses and worries in life. Of course, this is still the case when saved and in the ministry. The world is fickle, therefore our lives must be based on solid ground, knowing that Jesus loves us, we are forgiven, our worth is in Him, and we are heaven bound. When everything else is so quickly blown away, God and His Word still stand.

Our attitudes and values will be tested time and time again as our lives, friendships and ministries have peaks and troughs. Our prayer should always be that God would help us keep a right heart. We must never get caught up measuring our worth by comparing our financial position or the size of our church. The life and friendships of a pastor's wife must be based on higher things like God's principles of grace, love and acceptance. For His church to be built in the city in which we minister, each couple must follow their specific destiny and journey with God.

Mark 16:15 (NKJV)
And He said to them, "Go into all the world and preach the gospel to every creature."

Keeping our focus on spreading the gospel, as we are commanded, and on spiritual things will help us. We are an example of right priorities to our churches, to our families and a testimony to those not in church, whether in the workplace, community or school. We should always pray for friends and other ministering families, who might appear well outwardly, but could be struggling or working through hidden things.

May 23rd – *Athaliah's Words*

Y1 – Num 9 & 10 / Y2 – Heb 1 & 2

Let me guess; the morning alarm has gone off, your hair is a mess and you're plodding downstairs with one eye open and desperate for a coffee!! *Sound about right?*

2 Chronicles 22:3 (NKJV)
He (Ahaziah) walked in the ways of the house of Ahab and his mother (Athaliah) advised him to do wickedly!

Queen Athaliah's words of advice to her son were 'wicked' and later on in scripture we find that they completely derailed him. When Ahaziah dies, his mother Athaliah aggressively takes over as queen. The people of Israel rally together in a coup d'état and put Joash on the throne in her place. This upset Queen Athaliah greatly, so she throws a tantrum, rips her robes, and yells, 'Treason! Treason!' After her manifestation, the local people dragged her out onto the streets and killed her.

Have you ever advised (or your bad example has encouraged) your child to do wickedly?

This may be an extreme example, but we must be careful what we say, especially around children. When they say something 'wrong,' check yourself and ask if they are only repeating what they have heard. Did they learn that from me? Correct them with words that are constructive and not belittling.

Growing up, my mum would often tell me to control my tongue and never use unhelpful words like 'shut up,' 'crap,' or call someone names. Don't get me wrong, I've slipped up over the years. However, I have always felt a strong conviction and need to repent when I have spoken wrongly. I believe this conviction was partly due to a righteous mother's influence.

Lastly, remember that it is never too late for you to apologise to your children about the way you have conducted yourself in the past and repent of wrongdoing. An apology can often be the beginning of a transformation.

God help me! I don't want to stay the same! Unravel a seared conscience and cause me to grow in your character. Help me control my words and live a life that inspires my children to love and serve you! Amen.

May 24th – *Always Hope*

Y1 – Num 11 & 12 / Y2 – Heb 3 & 4

Psalms 106: 40, 43-45 (NKJV)
Therefore the wrath of the Lord was kindled against His people, so that He abhorred His own inheritance ... Many times He delivered them; But they rebelled in their counsel, and were brought low for their iniquity. Nevertheless He regarded their affliction, When He heard their cry; And for their sake He remembered His covenant, and relented according to the multitude of His mercies.

This Psalm is an overview of the history of Israel and God's patience and mercy towards them. My mind goes back to a conversation I had with another pastor's wife. We were speaking about people who, after experiencing trauma in their life still don't get saved. I said, 'If these things don't cause them to come to Jesus, then I don't think anything will! I mean, what else can God do?' She quickly replied, 'There is always hope.' When I read this scripture I thought the same thing, 'There is always hope!' This text is a perfect picture of God's love to the backslider. Even though they fight, run from God, and trample the grace they have received, when they call upon Him again, He remembers His covenant with them and His mercies come in multitudes.

Do you personally have hope for the broken and the backslidden? Do you pray for them?

We can sometimes become so caught up working with those in our church that we lose sight of the sheep who have wandered. God doesn't forget! My challenge to you this week is to get in touch with someone who has backslidden or drifted away and speak to them in love. Kind words and friendship go a long way.

Maybe you have not forgotten the people who have fallen away. Maybe your heart has been broken in the process of faithfully loving, sharing the gospel and accepting these people into your family. Do not let that hurt hinder your hope for them. Don't forget that Jesus is married to the backslider and is willing to finish the work He has begun in them. After all, His love for them is greater than ours.

Lord, I pray you will help me this week to speak to (insert name of person God has laid on your heart), be a friend they need, and to love them. Give me the words to say, touch them, and bring them back to Your love. I'm so thankful that you don't forget Your covenant with us. Amen.

May 25th – *Historical Women*
Y1 – Num 13 & 14 / Y2 – Heb 5 & 6

Rosa Parks (1913-2005)

Rosa Parks was born in Tuskegee, Alabama during a time of deep segregation in America. As a young African-American, she soon saw the inequalities. Black children had to walk to their underfunded schools, while school buses took white students to their new school fully stocked with books. Rosa's family were Christians, members of the African Methodist Episcopal Church, and prayer and the Bible were a part of her everyday life growing up.

Rosa later married, was an active member of the church, and became active in civil rights. On 1 December 1955, Rosa boarded the bus as usual after work, paid her fare, and sat in the first row of seats in the 'coloured' section at the back. The driver noticed several white passengers standing because their section was full so he moved the 'coloured' sign behind Rosa's row and demanded the four black people to surrender their seats. The other three did, but Rosa refused, saying, 'I don't think I should have to stand up.' The police were called, Rosa was arrested and later released.[1]

'I instantly felt God give me the strength to endure whatever would happen next,' she recounted. 'God's peace flooded my soul, and my fear melted away. All people were equal in the eyes of God, and I was going to live like a free person... People always say that I didn't give up my seat because I was tired... No, the only tired I was, was tired of giving in.'[2]

This event sparked the bus boycott in Alabama, which lasted over a year and led to nationwide victories to end racial segregation. Racism did not disappear just because segregation was no longer legal, but things slowly started to improve.

Rosa faced much hardship, losing employment and having multiple death threats, but her enduring love for the Lord and people saw her through every trial. It was the love of Christ in her that enabled her to fight for equal rights amongst different races.

May 26th – *Testimony*

Y1 – Ps 41 / Y2 – Ps 145

Soul Shaken by Anon

I've lived in my house for three years. Every week, without fail, I've watched a very slim, bleach blonde lady walk to the corner shop to buy her alcohol fix. She is undoubtedly an alcoholic and probably a drug user. My heart breaks for her and I constantly feel challenged to share the gospel with her. I have the answer for her, but I don't have the courage.

When the COVID-19 lockdown began, I was praying for her and God spoke to me, 'What is it going to take for you to speak to her? Does she have to die for you to realise her great need?'

I spoke to a friend about my fears and she graciously encouraged me to keep a church flier handy because it can be a good conversation starter for when I see her. Since then, I have been prepared to run out of the door at any given moment to witness and invite her to church, but sadly, four months have gone by and I haven't seen her.

What if she is dead?

I have always battled with witnessing for a variety of reasons. The fact that God's Word clearly and consistently says that we are to be soul winners has always plagued me. I know there is no higher calling and I strongly desire it, but can never seem to get past the mental block.

Why? Well, I've finally concluded that it's spiritual and something that I need to fight for. So let the fight begin!

When we pray, God gets involved. Something broke within me when God spoke to me about the lady on my road. I suddenly felt like her life depended on *my* witness (not my husband's). The fact that I still haven't seen her has genuinely shaken me. I know that God can move beyond me, but I *know* that she is my responsibility.

I write with tears in my eyes because the Lord has changed a part of me that I could not! For the first time in my life, I see souls… everywhere!

May 27th – *Study & Sermon Notes*

Y1 – Ps 42 / Y2 – Ps 146

May 28th – *Shimmering Saint*
Y1 – Num 15 & 16 / Y2 – Heb 7 & 8

1 Corinthians 1:2 (NKJV)
... to those who are sanctified in Christ Jesus, called to be saints, with all who in every place call on the name of Jesus Christ our Lord, both theirs and ours.

A saint in the Bible doesn't refer to a pious or revered person, canonised by an ecclesiastical body. It refers to all who have been consecrated, set apart and declared Holy! That's you! You were a sinner... now you are a saint! A born again believer!

When you accepted Christ and turned from old habits, God wrenched you out of the miry clay where your feet were firmly entrenched, where your muddled mind was a mess, and then He put you in a place of stability. By a miracle you were no longer stuck.

Just like in a classroom, where the naughty children are asked to move to the back so they won't be a bad influence, God separated you. He wanted to make sure you were protected so that you wouldn't be hurt, damaged, or influenced by sin again. Sanctified and set apart by God's grace!

Ephesians 2:19 (NIV)
Consequently, you are no longer foreigners and strangers, but fellow citizens with God's people and also members of his household,

God is kind. He could see that need for separation long before you did. Before you were walking in darkness, but now shining in His glorious light because you have been redeemed by His blood. Born into a new life and family, graciously changed and blessed!

Father God, I thank You for finding me and putting me in a place of stability. Help me to appreciate all You have done for me and to remember that I am a new creation in You, no longer living a life of sin, but one that pleases You as a saint.

May 29th – *Your Talents*
Y1 – Num 17 & 18 / Y2 – Heb 9 & 10

Exodus 4:2-5 (ESV)
The LORD said to him, "What is that in your hand?" He said, "A staff." And he said, "Throw it on the ground." So he threw it on the ground, and it became a serpent, and Moses ran from it. But the LORD said to Moses, "Put out your hand and catch it by the tail"—so he put out his hand and caught it, and it became a staff in his hand— "that they may believe that the LORD, the God of their fathers, the God of Abraham, the God of Isaac, and the God of Jacob, has appeared to you."

The staff is more than a shepherd's rod, it represents the identity, income and influence of Moses. God tells Moses to lay it down and, after it becomes a snake, to pick it back up. From this point on, God used this staff to work miracles in Egypt, part the Red Sea, bring water from a rock, and lead the people into freedom.

As a graphic designer, creating is part of who I am, how I make money, and how I wield influence. I've learnt that it's not about me, and if I try to make it about me, I quickly run out of inspiration. But when I lay it down and use it for God, there's a unique flow of ideas, a fountain of never-ending inspiration, new skills to learn, and things I could never imagine for myself.

Are you willing to lay it down so God can make it come to life, and work wonders in the world?

Sometimes it's hard to lay down the things we hold the closest or the things we feel identify us. However, God only asks this of us so He can take it and transform it into something even better for the purpose of His Kingdom. After all, every good and perfect gift comes from the Lord.

May 30th – *Have Discretion*
Y1 – Num 19 & 20 / Y2 – Heb 11 & 12

Proverbs 8:12 (NKJV)
I, wisdom, dwell with prudence, and find out knowledge and discretion.

Prudence is defined as behaviour that is careful and avoids risks.[1] Discretion has several definitions, which include the quality of being discreet with words or actions and the ability to behave in a way that does not cause offence.[2] These things accompany wisdom, which is given by God and also learnt from Him.

Proverbs 11:22 (NIV)
Like a gold ring in a pig's snout is a beautiful woman who shows no discretion.

The Amplified Version says, 'her lack of character mocks her beauty.' You can imagine a beautiful woman, a pastor's wife even, whose outward beauty is marred by gossip, negative words and rudeness that causes offence to those around her.

Matthew 12:36 (NKJV)
But I say to you that for every idle word men may speak, they will give account of it in the day of judgment.

A part of discretion is knowing what should be spoken, when, and to whom. That little piece of information we have been entrusted with, about a person doesn't need to be shared with others. Even if it seems like a harmless story we are conveying to family, friends, or fellow pastor's wives, we don't have to identify the characters by name. Idle words and gossip will cause people to lose trust in us and hurt those involved.

A woman with discretion is attractive, has influence for good, and people are drawn to her. We should all contend for this characteristic in our lives.

Father, I thank you for the truths in Your Word. I confess that there have been times I have been unwise in my conversation, with my words. I ask your Holy Spirit to help me pause to consider my words and weigh their value. Forgive me for the times I have spoken without wisdom. Help me have the courage to go back to that sister or brother to ask their forgiveness. Amen

May 31st – *That's It!*
Y1 – Num 21 & 22 / Y2 – Heb 13

One day, I arose early to get hold of God for the day and when I walked downstairs, I found that my living room looked a little disturbed. I knew I hadn't left the curtains open and cushions on the floor, nevertheless, I overlooked it, spent time with the Lord in prayer, and then got the children ready. Heading out the door, I reached for the keys and saw that they weren't on the key rack. Interesting! I looked out of my bay window and realised the car was gone. We had been robbed! Thieves had entered my house in the middle of the night, took my keys, and driven off down the road. I was shocked to say the least, but not fearful.

This was not the first time the devil had tried to intimidate me when my husband had gone away to preach, but I was sure it would be the last. That's it!

2 Tim 1:7 (NKJV)
For God has not given us a spirit of fear...

John 10:10 (NIV)
The thief comes only to steal and kill and destroy; I have come that they may have life and have it to the full.

Luke 10:19 (NIV)
I have given you authority to trample on snakes and scorpions and to overcome all the power of the enemy; nothing will harm you.

I hadn't spent over a decade internalising the Word of God for all of it to go out of the window when standing in the face of adversity. It was on His word I could lean during an attack. The foundation that we have built in Jesus means that we have been equipped for 'such a time as this.' Christians are not immune from trouble, but we are covered by a supernatural protection. Trials come to everybody, but it is much better to face a problem with God than without Him. Do not just roll over and accept troubles, put on the *whole* armour of God. Jesus gives you authority over the enemy so your life can be overflowing with goodness.

Time to purchase your next Devotional book

Volume 3

July – August - September

June 1st – *Jehovah M'Kadesh*

Y1 – Num 23 & 24 / Y2 – SOS 1 & 2

Leviticus 20 :7-8 (NKJV)
Consecrate yourselves therefore, and be holy, for I am the Lord your God. And you shall keep My statutes, and perform them: I am the Lord who sanctifies you.

Jehovah M'kaddesh is translated as 'the Lord who sanctifies.'[1] The Hebrew word is also translated as dedicate, consecrate and holy. The primary meaning is to be set apart or separate.

Genesis 2:3 (NKJV)
Then God blessed the seventh day and sanctified it, because in it He rested from all His work which God had created and made.

The Sabbath is a good example. It was set apart from other days in the week because it was to be different, holy, dedicated as belonging to God.[2]

1 Peter 1:15-16 (NKJV)
... But as He who called you is holy, you also be holy in all *your* conduct, because it is written, "Be holy, for I am holy."

As a holy God, He demands holiness from us. We will never measure up to God's holiness, yet by His grace we are made holy, set apart for His glory. What Jehovah was to His people in the Old Testament, as Jehovah the Holy One who sanctifies, the Lord Jesus Christ is in the New Testament.[3]

Hebrews 10:10 (NKJV)
By that will we have been sanctified through the offering of the body of Jesus Christ once for all.

Through Jesus we have salvation and are sanctified, yet we must continue to strive to be set apart and separate from the world and the influence of those around us. God gives us the tools to empower us to be a dedicated vessel for Him. His word and the Holy Spirit will reveal areas and truth in our lives.[4]

2 Corinthians 3:18 (NKJV)
But we all, with unveiled face, beholding as in a mirror the glory of the Lord, are being transformed into the same image from glory to glory, just as by the Spirit of the Lord.

We see change in our lives as we aim to become holy and more Christ like.

June 2nd – *Testimony*

Y1 – Ps 43 / Y2 – Ps 147

Salvation Story by Becky

I grew up in what may be described today as a normal family consisting of my mum, dad, brother and me. I started smoking as a teenager, getting drunk, going to parties, and being involved in relationships with boys; all things I also thought the norm.

As time went by, I wouldn't just get drunk, but began to experiment with drugs. At first it was weed, but then speed and cocaine. I didn't feel like I was ever addicted, just looking for an escape. An escape from what you may ask. I didn't even consciously know, but it wasn't working! I would get drunk and often have panic attacks. I had multiple sexual relationships, even with men much older than me. I was giving my body away in hope of finding love, searching for acceptance, but ending up feeling used and of low self-worth.

I moved 300 miles away from home to university, but continued on the same path I had been at home. Then, nearing the end of my first year at university, my friend invited me to a gospel concert. I had no idea what it would be like, but I decided to go with her. I sat through the music and testimonies, and when the altar call came I felt like a spotlight was being shined on me. I finally realised that for all those years there had been such an emptiness in my heart, a void that nothing I tried had the ability to fill. That day I prayed a prayer that changed the course of my life forever; I accepted Jesus Christ into my heart to be my Lord and Saviour. I felt forgiven, healed and loved.

It's been 13 years since Jesus stretched out his arms to me. I feel extremely blessed with a wonderful husband and three amazing children. I have experienced such joy, blessing and breakthroughs. None of it has been possible without Jesus guiding, challenging, and shaping me into a woman that reflects Him. The course of life has not always been easy, but no matter what, my hope and my faith lie in Jesus! My Rock, my Fortress, my Redeemer.

Psalm 91:4 (NLT)
He will cover you with his feathers. He will shelter you with his wings. His faithful promises are your armour and protection.

This my favorite verse. I picture a little bird going back to its mother in its nest, she's comforted, she's warm, she's safe. She knows that she's protected. This is my understanding of God. His promises are an arm wrapped around me, the encouragement in times of weariness and the rest in a place of refuge. In Him I will prosper!

June 3rd – *Study & Sermon Notes*

Y1 – Ps 44 / Y2 – Ps 148

June 4th – *Eighteen Inches*
Y1 – Num 25 & 26 / Y2 – SOS 3 & 4

Isaiah 64:6 (NKJV)
But we are all like an unclean *thing*, and all our righteousnesses *are* like filthy rags; We all fade as a leaf, and our iniquities, like the wind, have taken us away.

After I had been saved for a year or so, I ran across a tract that said you could miss heaven by 18 inches, which is the average distance between the head and the heart. The gravity of that statement summed up my life in a nutshell.

The thing that had separated me from Jesus Christ was my self-righteous head knowledge. I must admit, as a new convert I struggled with 'why' exactly I needed to be saved; after all, I had never killed anyone. I mean, I was all for going to heaven, but me, a sinner? This tract made me realise I had a form of godliness, but rejected its power, and the Bible says to avoid people like me. Wow, that was tough to swallow! Although I thought I possessed all these great qualities, they were like filthy rags compared to the holiness of Jesus.

I wish I could say that my self-righteousness is long buried and grace is always my immediate response to my fellow sojourners, but I'd be lying. Despite all I've been forgiven of and the fact that Jesus accepted me just as I am, I still struggle with being judgmental. I expect people to act more like me, think like me, be more level headed like me. It's quite embarrassing when I think about how many times I've had these thoughts. I know the further we travel along our journey, the closer we *should* be getting to Jesu, becoming more gracious, more understanding, and in everything becoming more like Him. I have moments of being Christlike, but honestly, they just remind me how far I have to go. Then again that is exactly what we need, to be reminded of those 18 inches that once separated us from the saving grace of Jesus.

Lamentations 3:22-23 (ESV)
The steadfast love of the Lord never ceases; his mercies never come to an end; they are new every morning; great is your faithfulness.

Thank you Lord, that I am covered in a robe of righteousness and you see Jesus in me. I please your blood over my mind and my thoughts. Let my thoughts and motives honour you and reflect your love for others. Amen.

June 5th – *God's Plan*

Y1 – Num 27 & 28 / Y2 – SOS 5 & 6

Genesis 12:5 (NKJV)
Then Abram took Sarai his wife ...

This story is a good illustration of how Sarah followed Abraham and trusted in God, that He would provide for all her needs and for her future. We have followed our husbands into ministry, not knowing which way we were going or what the future holds, but believing and trusting God. Sarah's story gives us the expectation that God's plans include us as wives.

Proverbs 16:9 (NKJV)
A man's heart plans his way, but the LORD directs his steps.

Throughout my Christianity, I have experienced many miracles that have shown me God was leading and directing my steps. I came back to the UK from Australia with no friends or church. I visited every church in the area over several months. Finally, God brought me to The Potter's House, where the pastor at that time was Australian. I had been so down because I missed Australia, but God gave me a blessing in the form of an Australian family to love.

When we went out to pioneer, God gave my husband a specific location to open the church. In that same area, we miraculously had houses to rent and then one to buy, and my children's schooling needs were met. God showed me His goal is to build the church and that His plan *includes* providing for the minister's family.

Many years later, we were moving to take over a church. I was house hunting in a specific area due to schooling and the only available house at that time had a small gravel garden. I was honestly frustrated with God that we didn't have a 'proper' garden. My husband then got cancer, so obviously would have been unable to mow the lawn like normal. I felt so relieved that we didn't have a garden that needed mowing! God revealed to me that in our obedience, there is always a blessing.

While praying, open your heart to God's blessing and know He always has a plan.

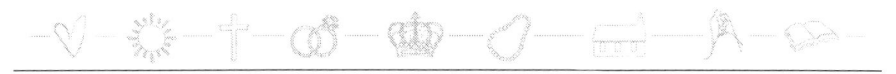

June 6th – *Scrolls & Parchments*

Y1 – Num 29 & 30 / Y2 – SOS 7 & 8

2 Timothy 4:13 (NIV)
When you come, bring the cloak that I left with Carpus at Troas, and my scrolls, especially the parchments.

Paul is in prison and asks his trusted friend Timothy to bring him some essentials: a warm coat, parchments and his scrolls. In Bible times, scriptures were written on papyrus paper, rolled around a stick, and then bound together with some rope. Now I don't know about you, but if I was in prison I wouldn't even be able to make out the words on a scroll because I would be crying so much 'Get me out of here!' This was clearly not the case for Paul, with no time for self-pity, he knuckled down and got to reading.

When was the last time you read a book?

Why read? Reading 1) stimulates the mind, 2) reduces stress, 3) increases knowledge, 4) expands vocabulary, 5) improves memory, 6) develops analytical skills, 7) improves concentration, 8) hones writing skills, 9) maintains calm, and 10) provides entertainment.[1]

Isaac Newton once wrote, 'If I have seen further, it is by standing on the shoulders of giants.'[2] Newton ascribes his success and intellect to those who had gone before him. Books are mostly written by people who have a great deal of time formulating their thoughts into words and making them accessible for our benefit. What would we do without the Bible? Solomon tells us that in a 'multitude of counsellors there is safety.'[3] Books often provide that counsel, so we must take advantage of them. I can't tell you the amount of times I have referred to a James Dobson book for help with raising my children.

Proverbs 4: 7 (NKJV)
Wisdom *is* the principal thing; *Therefore*, get wisdom. And in all your getting, get understanding.

How do you get wisdom and understanding? Read! This week, your challenge is to think of an area of your life you need assistance with, find a book on it, buy it or get it from the library, and read it (*all of it*).

June 7th – *Taking Authority*

Y1 – Num 31 & 32 / Y2 – James 1 & 2

2 Corinthians 10:4-5 (NIV)
The weapons we fight with are not the weapons of the world. On the contrary, they have divine power to demolish strongholds. We demolish arguments and every pretension that sets itself up against the knowledge of God, and we take captive every thought to make it obedient to Christ.

The memory I have of the first ladies' prayer meeting I ever attended is my pastor's wife laying on the map of the country where she had been a missionary and crying over it. She was (and still is to this day) a passionate woman of prayer.

I know of another woman who, faced with infidelity in her marriage, continued to be one of the first people at morning prayer. She knew it was only God that could carry her through that time.

I was reading about Terry Waite and of his 1,763 days (five years) being a hostage in Beirut. He could not read the Bible, had no fellowship, no sun, and no sky. He learnt the importance of the *now* concluding, 'There is a relationship between identity, language, and prayer; somehow they keep you together at your centre.'

Spiritual warfare rages against your family, your marriage and your church. The scriptures vocalised in prayer are your spiritual missiles. Be bold in your petitions and take authority in Jesus name.

Here are a few of verses I have memorised and spoken out in prayer: Isaiah 54:17, 2 Corinthians 10:4-5, and Hebrews 7:25. Why not write your own. Make them dear to you.

God will build His church! Speaking His word in prayer lays claim to His promises and works to pulling down the strongholds of the enemy!

The less we speak and the more we pray, means more of God's involvement and less of our meddling. Being still and disciplined to pray daily can be a challenge, but consider if you don't eat, how malnourished you become! Similarly, if you don't pray, you become an emaciated, weak, and self-driven Christian.

Sisters, there is power in your prayers, let it be your greatest legacy!

June 8th – *Light's On*
Y1 – Num 33 & 34 / Y2 – James 3 & 4

Matthew 5:14-16 (NLT)
You are the light of the world—like a city on a hilltop that cannot be hidden. No one lights a lamp and then puts it under a basket. Instead, a lamp is placed on a stand, where it gives light to everyone in the house. In the same way, let your good deeds shine out for all to see, so that everyone will praise your heavenly Father.

Every Christian is called to be a bright light. A light guides people and illuminates the path. Alternatively, darkness restricts people and causes them to stumble. Jesus is saying that the light of Christ in us should not be hidden, but we are to let it boldly shine for all to see, like a city on a hill or a lamp on a stand.

Where do you store the light of Christ? Is it out in the open or reserved in private?

As we know, part of letting our light shine is keeping a good testimony. Some have the headstrong mindset, 'People just need to take me as I am!' Others are snared by being overly concerned with what people think of them. We need to find our security in what Jesus thinks of us and strive to let our light shine before men so that Christ can be seen in us.

If we unapologetically conduct our lives according to God's Word, it be our guide about what we wear, what we listen to, what we say and what we do. People will take note that we are the 'real deal' and we will be an example of God's love and grace to the world around us.

What do people think (friends, family, ladies in your church) when your name is mentioned?

Proverbs tells us that a 'good name' is to be chosen.[1] The good news is, because of the Holy Spirit working in us, our light can grow stronger and stronger and we can be the beacon that leads another to salvation. Let's be a gospel billboard and advertise Jesus!

June 9th – *Testimony*

Y1 – Ps 45 / Y2 – Ps 149

Evangelist's Wife by Pam

Zechariah 4:10 (NLT)
Do not despise these small beginnings, for the LORD rejoices to see the work begin ...

Pastor Wayman Mitchell always placed a great deal of dignity on the local church. But it was not until I had the privilege as an evangelist's wife to visit churches throughout our Fellowship that I began to deeply appreciate just what that meant. For most of our churches, they are working hard to emulate and reproduce the success of their mother church or one of our 'bigger' Fellowship churches. This is the admirable and natural desire of every couple sent into the ministry. However, I have developed a newfound respect for the efforts and achievements of our pioneer pastors, their wives, and our 'smaller' works.

Some of the most generous, warm-hearted people and spirit-filled, anointed worship services that I have been blessed to experience, have been in churches that may be regarded as 'small' in numbers, location and profile. God shows no partiality regarding these factors. I have felt the tangible presence of God in these works, and it was evident they were implementing and contending for everything they had learnt in their mother church: disciples are risen up, world vision is instilled, and evangelism is at the heart and centre of what is taught.

I would like to commend all pioneer pastors and their wives for doing a great job upholding an honourable calling and recognise the dignity in what they are trying to establish. Pastor Mitchell taught us that it isn't about numbers, but it's about souls. We know this isn't an excuse for our churches not to grow, or for them to rest on their laurels once they've reached a certain size, but it is an acknowledgment that God is not a respecter of persons, and that He moves in any setting, anywhere, at any time. There are many pioneer works, or what would be considered 'smaller' churches, that are impacting their local communities, being a blessing to other Fellowship churches around them, and making a difference in the lives of the members of their congregations.

I encourage all pioneer works and smaller churches not to be demoralized by low 'numbers, nickels or noise.' Your worth is not measured by having a slick building or the latest cutting-edge technology. Do not allow discouragement and frustration to be your armour bearers. Once you have the Spirit of God, a heart for people, and are doing all that you have been taught to do, you have a lot! God will be faithful to add the rest.

Sharing the good news

Of myself I am not able
To fulfil my Lord's command.
Only in Christ do I have the power
To love my fellowman.

He gives me strength to speak to them,
And tell them that God is love
And that He came to die for them
Reconciling to God above.

For the love of God goes deeper
Than the depths of sin and shame
And the grace of God reaches out to all
Who call upon His name.

For there is power in the Name of Christ
And love beyond all measure
To every child of Adam's race
Who would obtain the Treasure.

But I must be the hand of God
Stretched out to those in sin
And I must work while it is day
To bring the wanderer in.

by Gertrude Jefferies

June 10th - *Study & Sermon Notes*

Y1 – Ps 46 / Y2 – Ps 150

June 11th – *Supernatural Provision*

Y1 – Num 35 & 36 / Y2 – James 5

1 Kings 17:5-6 (NKJV)
So he went and did according to the word of the LORD, for he went and stayed by the Brook Cherith, which flows into the Jordan. The ravens brought him bread and meat in the morning, and bread and meat in the evening; and he drank from the brook.

Because Elijah believed the word of the Lord and acted on it, he experienced God's abundant grace and provision in the most unlikely manner. Ravens steal food naturally to survive, but God used them to provide for Elijah in the wilderness.

Many times when God calls us to ministry, we have to leave our comfort zones of security and financial stability, and step out into the unknown. It is then, as we trust God and obey by faith, that we are able to experience God's sustaining power. As with the ravens, He is able to bring us resources from places we never thought possible.

One such experience that stands out to me is when our eldest child was about to start school. It was the weekend before and we had nothing ready. We had decided to make a financial sacrifice for our summer outreaches, so my husband was on an impact team and I was home with the children. It was around 6pm, I was in the living room, curled up on the sofa with the children, crying out desperately to God for miracle finances, when the doorbell rang. I opened the door and there was a lady from church with bags from Marks & Spencer. She was sent by a dear sister who occasionally came to church, but was not generally involved. In those bags were everything our daughter needed for school, and more. I just broke down in tears, in awe of God's provision! God sees you and your circumstances and He will come through for you. Step out in faith and trust Him.

Thank you Lord that I do not need to be anxious for anything, that I can bring all things to you in prayer, with thanksgiving. Thank you for your peace which surpasses all understanding, for your love and care for me. Amen.

June 12th – *Many Poor*

Y1 – 1 Cor 1 & 2 / Y2 – Isa 1 & 2

Galatians 2 :10 (NKJV)
They desired only that we should remember the poor, the very thing which I also was eager to do.

Matthew 26:11 (NKJV)
For you have the poor with you always…

Almost half the world, over three billion people, live on less than $2.50 a day, nearly a billion people entered the 21st century unable to read a book, and sadly 2.2 million children die each year because they have not been immunised.

I live in a very large city where 37% of children live in deep poverty and 8,330 families live in overcrowded homes. People who live under the poverty line are more likely to suffer from mental health issues, be exposed to sexual, physical or mental abuse. They are less likely to get a good education that opens a door to opportunity, are more likely to have drug or alcohol addictions, and are more likely to commit a crime.

Do you think about the poor? How do you approach them? Do you love them?

The poor hold a special place in the heart of Jesus. The Bible says they are 'rich in faith', because their great need causes them to turn to God and depend on Him for their provisions.

Contrast this with those who trust in their wealth. A rich young ruler came to Jesus and asked, 'What must I do to be saved?' Jesus replies, 'One thing you lack, go, sell everything you have and give to the poor, and you will have treasure in heaven.' This man walks away, sad, because he had great possessions. Following Jesus is costly, but unbeknownst to those who reject Him, what we gain is far greater and longer lasting than what money can ever buy.

Salvation isn't based on our works, nor on how much money we do or don't have. We will all stand before our Saviour one day and await His judgment. He will consider how we treated the poor, and our attitude towards possessions. We must trust in Him supremely and hold on to what He values.

June 13th – *Order, Order!*
Y1 – 1 Cor 3 & 4 / Y2 – Isa 3 & 4

1 Corinthians 14:33 (NLT)
For God is not a God of disorder but of peace, as in all the meetings of God's holy people.

God created the cycles of nature as a perfect example of order in which things efficiently operate, in perfection. Likewise, embracing order within our home can help us function effectively and promote a peaceful atmosphere. Taking each day as it comes causes chaos and confusion, especially when you add the pressures of ministry to the everyday stresses of life. I have learnt this the hard way.

Once, my daughter informed me at 8:00am that very day that she was having a dress-up day at school and needed a costume. The feeling of panic and stress was not enjoyable and totally avoidable if I had read the school newsletter.

Order requires self-discipline to get things done as planned, yet it ensures our time and resources are used in the best possible way. Instead of living in a flurry of badly planned survival strategies, we can use order to approach everything with excellence, giving the best of ourselves.

Does your day (or week) contain order and routine? Is your planning effective, realistic and working efficiently? Are you on the same page as your husband? Do your individual schedules collide or compliment each other?

Now, I know what you are thinking. From sister to sister it undoubtedly needs to be said that even with calendars, meal plans, rotas and charts, continental order is not achievable. We have a limited amount of time and energy, therefore prioritising what is important as it letting other things go. *What are your priorities?* Some things may be a good idea. Some things you could complete better than those currently in charge, but does that really matter? Would it take time away from things that are more important? Prioritising is a gift of time-management to yourself and contributes to your peace of mind.

God help me to identify where in my life I need more order. Help me find ways to embrace self-discipline and organise my time. Help me consider the right priorities so I can give the best of my time and energy to Your work.

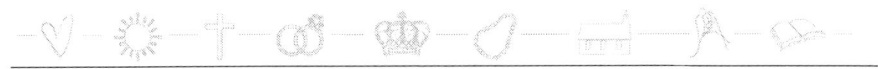

June 14th – *Open Doors*

Y1 – 1 Cor 5 & 6 / Y2 – Isa 5 & 6

Revelation 3:7-8 (NKJV)
"And to the angel of the church in Philadelphia write, 'These things says He who is holy, He who is true, "He who has the key of David, He who opens and no one shuts, and shuts and no one opens": "I know your works. See, I have set before you an open door, and no one can shut it; for you have a little strength, have kept My word, and have not denied My name."

The open door from God in this instance indicates an opportunity to advance God's kingdom because of the church in Philadelphia's faithfulness.[1] Ellicott's and Matthew Henry's commentary says the open door was not simply a way of escape from difficulties, but an opening for preaching the gospel and an opportunity of doing good.[2]

This scripture clearly states that a door opened by God cannot be closed by anyone. We can pray for God to open doors which can bring clarity and peace to a situation and help us when in a crossroads of life. An open door might appear from God as an opportunity and be confirmed in multiple ways, but it will always line up with His Word.[3] Often an open door might not present in the way we expect, but we can evaluate it through prayer, wise counsel and His Word. We might have to test and push doors to see which one opens and where God is moving us.

My fellow pastor's wife, do not allow the enemy to persuade you that serving in the ministry is all about sacrifice that restricts and suffocates you. Fill your heart with faith and trust the Lord to open doors of blessing for you!

Lord, help me be open and receptive to the different opportunities you have for me, that I would respond in the correct manner. In this area (speak it out! For example decisions in ministry, house hunting, etc.) I need you to open or close doors as you see fit. Give guidance concerning Your will for our lives. Amen.

June 15th – *Mystery Revealed*

Y1 – 1 Cor 7 & 8 / Y2 – Isa 7 & 8

Ephesians 3 :4-5 (NLV)
When you read this, you will understand how I know about the things that are not easy to understand about Christ. Long ago men did not know these things. But now they have been shown to His missionaries and to the early preachers by the Holy Spirit.

Although God has a perfect and detailed plan for our lives, it isn't always clear to us what it is. At times, we think we know what God wants us to do, and other times we haven't the foggiest! In the NKJV, the heading over these verses is "The Mystery Revealed" because Paul is highlighting that in the current dispensation of time, the mystery of Christ is being presented to us.

We don't have all the answers. As a matter of fact, sometimes we don't even know the right questions to ask. However, while serving God in the present, He will reveal His plans for us. Jesus promised that the Spirit of Truth would be our guide and that He will tell us of things to come.[1] My husband heard from God through the Holy Spirit (verse 5) about pioneering a church on the other side of the country and we knew we had to obey. We were unsure of what was waiting for us, but the longer we serve, the more God is building, not only His church, but also our faith, and our marriage. His plans are slowly, but surely being revealed to us. We are unable to understand all God's plans for us up-front, so He often gives them to us piece by piece. There is a saying 'the long term saints see the long term miracles'. This is so true. If you stick around, you will see the Lord unfold His mysterious plans and blessing in and through your life, something you certainly don't want to miss.

Yes, the unknown can be frustrating! It's best not to focus and obsess over the big plans of the future. Only God knows them. Concentrate on following and obeying Jesus in the here and now. Trust that one day those promises shall be revealed.

June 16th – *Testimony*

Y1 – Ps 47 / Y2 – Jer 1

Salvation Story by Charlotte

I was born into a Christian home. My parents pioneered a church for several years, but eventually returned home to the mother church for some recuperation. Sadly, after some time, my parent's relationship broke down and my father walked away from Jesus. It was a tough time, nevertheless, my parents were faithful to provide and to love us.

Through it all, my brothers and I witnessed our mother's unquenchable joy and love that only Jesus can give. She was our solid, godly role model. She continued to faithfully attend church, pray, and serve. Her example gave me hope in a time of despair.

My mum and dad eventually got divorced, but to this day I have never heard them put each other down, argue or fight over us. Their conduct was mature and I am so grateful for it. However, there was a time that I found their civil behaviour confusing and abnormal. 'Why are mum and dad so kind to each other, surely they should be arguing?' Unable to make sense of it, the emotions of frustration and anger slowly ate away at me and subtly infiltrated into other parts of my life.

All of my peers at school knew that I was a Christian and loved Jesus. I stood for righteousness, spoke against abortion, wore modest clothing, declined the many worldly party invitations, and encouraged my friends to stay pure. Many would ask me for my advice and I would say, 'Are you willing to hear my Christian advice?' They often did. As an adolescent, I prayed that I would be 'all things to all men'[1] like Paul. God heard my cry and, by a miracle, I built relationships with all types of people in school (i.e. trendies, townies, goths, the tough girls and the poorest kids) It was truly a blessing to know them all, each wonderful in their own way. To the world I looked like a saint, but God saw my heart and it was becoming quite a mess.

Coupled with frustration and anger, I also started climbing the ladder of pride. I struggled with the concept of sin, after all, what had I done? I loved people, genuinely served in church, and with all my heart desired God. Yet, I started to adopt the kind of attitude that I believe church kids are prone to, one of arrogance.

Church kids are typically talented (because of being involved in ministries from a young age), loved (because the church has watched us grow up), looked up to, hands on, able to communicate with people of all back grounds, and confident. This 'what have I ever done' mentality combined with my internal frustration, was a perfect recipe for a fall.

At age seventeen, I got into a relationship that I believed was 'divine destiny.' I was smitten, yet blind! My church kid arrogance wouldn't allow me to listen to the warning signs or the words of people around me. On one occasion, after dating for about a year, I found myself in a compromising situation. It was enough to thoroughly shake me. Ashamed and broken, I was forced to face the truth about the pain in my life and accept responsibility for my actions.

From that moment on I knew what it meant to be a sinner. I now understand that it was a disease I was born with and one only Jesus Christ could set me free. I am so blessed to have been humbled at that time in my life and, funnily enough, I knew it was exactly what I needed. Even in that time of lesson and pain, I consciously glorified my Jesus knowing that He was the only one who would get me through it. It is so much better to go through hardships with God than without Him. "For I know the plans I have for you," says the LORD. "They are plans for good and not for disaster, to give you a future and a hope."[2]

The following years were tough. I worked through endless mind battles, but still I realised how blessed I was because I had a church, a loving family and best of all, Jesus. There was a season that I felt desperate to be loved by a man, get married, and 'do God's will.' I failed to realise at the time that God had a will for me besides my dreams of marriage. Slowly, I began to recognise I subconsciously depended on people to provide my happiness and not God. Was I genuinely content? No. Did I actually trust God with my future? Sometimes. Was I willing to let my life unfold how God wanted without my constant manipulation? Eventually the answer was *yes*! Fed up with myself and my lack, I chose to pray, change and then act. The feeling of being dissatisfied drove me insane so the scripture, 'godliness with contentment is great gain'[3] became my anthem. Shortly after these revelations, my unrighteous, negative, and self-serving mindsets shifted and I began to feel whole.

Soon after this change, a fine young man from church asked me out on a date. We had known each other since I was seven, served God together in ministries for over 15 years, yet we had never considered each other to be anything more than friends. Until now, (possibly because I was too cool for him, although he would say the opposite). Sparks were flying! We tied the knot in a 'Jesus people' wedding Six months later. Soon after, we began our life's work in the ministry, which is an immense, life changing privilege.

June 17th - *Study & Sermon Notes*

Y1 – Ps 48 / Y2 – Jer 2

June 18th – *Clean Crib*

Y1 – 1 Cor 9 & 10 / Y2 – Isa 9 & 10

Proverbs 14:4 (NKJV)
Where there are no oxen, the manger is empty, but from the strength of an ox come abundant harvests.

Have you ever thought how your church would look if you ran it?

My friend and I were discussing this and one of the comments was, 'I doubt there would be anybody *in* the church if I was in charge!' We laughed at the thought of having no problems, but then agreed that without people the church would be colourless, lifeless and useless.

This proverb draws a lesson from the farm. Oxen require a lot of upkeep. If they weren't around the farmer wouldn't have to feed them, tend to their health, or clean up the mess they leave behind. However, the farmer would no longer benefit from their incredible strength and all that they accomplish. To this day they are used for riding, threshing grain by trampling, ploughing, transportation, and much more. They can bear a much heavier load than a horse and, although slower, they have more endurance.[1] Oxen were an essential part of a functioning farm in Biblical times.

We can apply this same lesson to saints in church. People can be messy, may put a strain on your emotions, and require investment of time and resources. Yet, they are the indispensable body of Christ and, truth be told, without them there would be no church.

Interestingly, oxen have been known to run away if they are pushed to their limits, as they can actually feel taken for granted.[2] Let this never be said for the men and women in our churches. Oxen have incredible power, and abilities few other animals possess. This is the same with precious saints in our congregations. With them, we experience true joy, witness transformed lives, and through impartation and discipleship, observe people soar into destiny. This vision is what brings immense strength to the church and its purpose. Therefore, we are to love and nourish them, realising the great blessing and value of God's people.

June 19th – *Emotionally Intimate*

Y1 – 1 Cor 11 & 12 / Y2 – Isa 11 & 12

Genesis 24:58 (NKJV)
Then they called Rebekah and said to her, "Will you go with this man?" And she said, "I will go."

Rebekah trusted her future husband Isaac and moved away from her family to marry him. We are pastor's wives and willing to follow our husbands, trusting their calling. But do you trust him with matters of the heart?

Intimacy is having a close union, being transparent, knowing everything about each other, and not holding back. In order to have an intimate relationship with our husbands we must trust them. How can we be intimately close without the regular sharing of our hearts, trusting them with our thoughts and feelings, connecting through discussion, and talking through things?

Being in the ministry will bring seasons of busyness, pressures, trials, and multiplied distractions. If we aren't careful, a few days go by where we and our husbands are passing like ships in the night, and before we know it, a distance is created. You feel like you have no idea what has been going on in your husband's day, what he is thinking or going through. If this isn't recognised and addressed, it can create a chasm so wide that lots of dedicated time and healing is required. We need to constantly cherish and nourish our spouse and marriage.

Of course, intimacy is also defined as part of a sexual relationship, which is so important to maintain. How can you be sexually intimate without being aware of each other emotionally? In a good marriage the couple wants to spend time together intimately.[1]

Songs of Solomon 8:14 (NKJV)
Make haste, my beloved, and be like a gazelle or a young stag on the mountains of spices.

This couple is desperate to be together, devote time to be emotionally connected, and reap the benefits of an intimate relationship.

Father, I give my marriage to you. I'm asking you to heal the wounds, equip me and show me how to nourish my marriage, and help me trust my husband with all that I am. Amen

June 20th – *Fort Knox*

Y1 – 1 Cor 13 & 14 / Y2 – Isa 13 & 14

2 Corinthians 10:5 (NIV)
We demolish arguments and every pretension that sets itself up against the knowledge of God, and we take captive every thought to make it obedient to Christ.

How often do your thoughts run away with you? How often do you find yourself creating scenarios that don't even exist? How often do you have imaginary conversations with someone who you'd like to give 'a piece of your mind?'

In this text, Paul is talking about spiritual warfare. I heard a pastor once say, 'Only when we get to heaven will we understand how spiritual life on earth is.' He is suggesting that we operate in the spiritual far more than we can comprehend. We wrestle against things unseen and have an invisible enemy shooting spiritual arrows, drenched in fire, intentionally aimed at causing an uncontrollable explosion in our minds, hearts, and emotions.

Women typically have an active mind, often over-thinking. We also tend to be more personal and sensitive. Whilst these characteristics are essential and useful, they do make us more vulnerable and prone to assaults of the mind.

If that's you, I've got a simple (but not easy) solution.

Put your negative thoughts into prison, lock the door, and throw the key away. You must learn to discern unrighteous or ungodly thoughts and practice rejecting them.

Fort Knox contains $184.7 million dollars of the world's finest gold. Therefore, it also has the world's finest, most intricate, security system. Your mind is spiritual gold and requires protection, otherwise, you will be robbed of a sound mind and be rendered unfit for purpose. We need to be mentally healthy.

Lord Jesus, sometimes I feel opposed, unloved, devalued, and my mind gets out of control. I recognise that I must be obedient to Your Word and believe the truth. You are the Creator of my mind and I'm believing You to help me discern Satan's fiery darts so that I don't permit my mind to go on a destructive rampage. I thank You for this continued deliverance. Amen.

June 21st – *Time out!*
Y1 – 1 Cor 15 & 16 / Y2 – Isa 15 & 16

Matthew 14 :3 (NKJV)
For Herod had laid hold of John and bound him and put him in prison ...

John the Baptist, the cousin of Jesus and the forerunner of His ministry, had been imprisoned and, subsequently, beheaded.

Mathew 14:13-14 (NKJV)
When Jesus heard it, He departed from there by boat to a deserted place by Himself. But when the multitudes heard it, they followed Him on foot from the cities. And when Jesus went out He saw a great multitude; and He was moved with compassion for them, and healed their sick.

We see Jesus was clearly moved by this horrible and cruel act. Perhaps He needed some time out, some respite, so He heads off by Himself, only to be followed by people who were in need.

How does Jesus respond to this interruption?

Christ's compassion compelled Him to heal, even though He had just been bereaved. This chapter goes on to record Jesus meeting the needs of the multitude and feeding five thousand men plus women and children. After this, He sends the disciples ahead and finally gets time alone on a mountain top.

We've all been there, trying to wrap our heads around personal, church, and ministry issues, pressed for time but faced with urgent needs. We often feel as though there is never any time for ourselves or our families to be refreshed. The truth is, we have to make time. Jesus was a 'man of sorrows, and acquainted with grief,' so He doesn't just demand that we get on with it in spite of our pain. He went to the Father because He needed that time, and so do we. He healed the sick, challenged the faith of the disciples by pressing them to step out and believe God for the impossible, and miraculously fed the multitude. However, He then made time to be refreshed in His Spirit.

Lord, forgive me for neglecting myself. I do not have the capacity to meet all the demands and carry the load without your help. Teach me to cast all my cares on you. Amen.

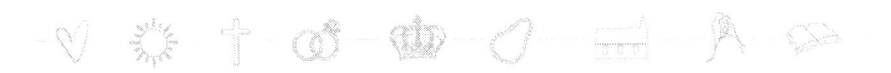

June 22nd – *Historical Women*
Y1 – Mal 1 & 2 / Y2 – Isa 17 & 18

Lilias Trotter (1852-1928)

Lilias was a gifted painter and her art was soon discovered by a famous artist named John Ruskin. As much as she loved painting, her real passion was traveling to London's Victoria Station to find outcasts and minister to them. She would take prostitutes in and look after them, keeping them safe for the night. She saw the conditions of working women and became instrumental in forming the first public restaurant for women in London.

She had a heart of love. John Ruskin admired it, but he thought it was a shame that she spent all her time helping others when she could be working on her art. He gave her an ultimatum: be the greatest female artist in England, or turn her back on that dream. Lilias realised she couldn't give herself to painting the way Ruskin wanted her to, so she rejected the idea of fame. She trusted in the Lord and continued to seek first His kingdom.

Lilias responded to a challenge for missionaries to go into North Africa, but the mission's board turned her down due to health reasons. However, because she had the resources to be self-supporting, they decided Lilias could work with two other women without officially being a member. So in March 1888, the three women left for the predominantly Islamic nation of Algeria.

Lilias said that the early years were like 'knocking our heads against stone walls,' but eventually Lilias gained access to the heavily secluded women by first befriending their children. She evangelised with 'a native cafe on a Christian footing,' readings of the Bible in a 'rhythmical recitative,' a craft house that would teach girls embroidery, and a Christian retreat for women to 'take the place of the outings to shrines which are their only chance of fresh air.'[1]

She died in 1928, but even during her last years, she fought for the women in Algeria. She is truly an inspiration; such strength, such a legacy.

June 23rd – *Testimony*

Y1 – Ps 49 / Y2 – Jer 3

God's Touch by Claire

2 Kings 5:14 (NKJV)
And his flesh was restored like the flesh of a little child, and he was clean.

This scripture is about Naaman's healing from leprosy. I love this Bible story because it describes his skin being completely and perfectly restored like that of a newborn. I can relate to Naaman's unclean condition and to the subsequent miracle that he experienced once he responded to God's call.

I grew up in a broken home. My parents were involved in a cult called The Children of God, which you may have heard of because of the repeatedly bad press it received due to thousands of allegations of sexual abuse. Unfortunately, I was one of many who were exposed to these violations.

For years I struggled with the labels and lies the enemy had sown in my heart, but when I learned to believe and apply the Truth I experienced a transformation. God spoke to me 'I have given you childlike innocence and purity', just like Naaman's skin that went from leprous to perfection. God showed me that we lack nothing in Christ, and He assured me I was not to blame myself for what happened. Over the years, I have read extensively about the effects of sexual interference on children and, whilst the implications are devastating, there is nothing the Cross of Christ can't deal with. When we repent of our own sin a process of sanctification begins. I can testify to healing, deliverance, and total freedom because of Jesus. It took time, but now I am free from shame, condemnation, insecurity, lust, anger and rejection. I have learnt to discern the lies of the enemy and distinguish what is true.

1 John 3.8 (ESV)
For this reason, Christ was revealed: to destroy all the works of the evil one.

If you have been hurt or are hurting, I want to encourage you, God can restore that which has been lost.

June 24th – *Study & Sermon Notes*

Y1 – Ps 50/ Y2 – Jer 4

June 25th – *God's Medicine*

Y1 – Mal 3 & 4 / Y2 – Isa 19 & 20

Proverbs 17:22 (NIV)
A cheerful heart is good medicine, but a crushed spirit dries up the bones.

The Bible prescribes a cheerful, merry or glad heart as medication for the spirit. We know medication is used to improve health conditions or illness, but it can also be used to prevent sickness. Could this be so with laughter? Think about what a merry heart could circumvent.

Laughter is often spontaneous and provoked by something one might find humorous. In life, we are often drawn to those who are funny and charismatic, only to find that their lives are empty and unfulfilled. Just because a person laughs doesn't mean they are filled with joy. Let this not be said of the Christian, let alone the wife of a pastor. Whilst her life can at times be filled with trials, stress and complications, I pray her example will remain an infectious, joyful one.

When was the last time you threw your head back and laughed?

Proverbs 31:25 (NLT)
She is clothed with strength and dignity, and she laughs without fear of the future.

One of the character traits of this virtuous wife is the ability to laugh. She isn't laughing because she has no worries, problems or pressures, but because she has the ability to put her troubles on a shelf (for a period of time) and enjoy life. She has a joy that stems from casting her cares on Him, by faith.

Romans 15:13 (NKJV)
Now may the God of hope fill you with all joy.

As Christians, we should be the happiest people on the planet because we have experienced salvation. Jesus has taken away all our guilt and shame and we are destined for eternity with Him.

Father, I ask you to fill my heart and life with joy and laughter. I sometimes feel exhausted and overwhelmed, forgetting the joy of the Lord is my strength.[1] I'm focused now on all I have to be grateful for and I am asking you to lift my spirit. Amen.

June 26th – *Few Needs*

Y1 – Deut 1 & 2 / Y2 – Isa 21 & 22

Luke 10:41-42 (NIV)
"Martha, Martha," the Lord answered, "you are worried and upset about many things, but few things are needed—or indeed only one. Mary has chosen what is better, and it will not be taken away from her."

I believe Martha reflects many women in the ministry. Here, she is opening her home and serving others, including Jesus, in her place, doing what she is supposed to be doing. In the culture of that day (and ours), Mary should have been helping her. However, Mary has chosen instead to sit and listen to Jesus, taking the posture of a student, which usually was reserved for men. This was irritating for Martha, who perhaps would also have preferred to have sat and listened to Jesus, but felt obligated to prepare the meal. Eventually, her frustration boils over and she complains to Jesus, no doubt confident that He would back her up. But instead He gently rebukes her, not because she was serving, but rather that she was worried and upset when it was not necessary. He tells her, 'few things are needed', and then narrows it down to, 'indeed only one.' This is what Mary has chosen.

We can often miss very important moments in our lives by being distracted with busyness. Often the expectations of others or the pressures we put on ourselves cause us to feel obligated to do certain things. This can lead us to neglect what God wants us to do. Perhaps we rush into the day without spending time in prayer, prioritise cleaning the house over spending valuable time with our children, or focus on the 'to do' list and miss the opportunity to reach out and share the Gospel with someone. Obviously we have responsibilities, but let us choose better like Mary did, trusting our Lord resulting in less frustration, anxiety, and leading to a more wholesome relationship with God and others.

Thank you, my loving Father, that you are able to make all grace abound towards me, that I may always have all sufficiency in all things and an abundance for every good work. Amen.

June 27th – *Sweet Sleep*
Y1 – Deut 3 & 4 / Y2 – Isa 23 & 24

Various studies worldwide have shown the prevalence of insomnia in 10%-30% of the population, some even as high as 50% – 60%. This is common in older adults, females, people with medical conditions and those with mental health issues.[1] For many, fear is the culprit. Anxiety and worry about finances, family members and health; the list is extensive and varies depending on our own individual fears and how we have been conditioned to process things.

Proverbs 3:24 (ESV)
If you lie down, you will not be afraid; when you lie down, your sleep will be sweet.

The Bible promises sweet sleep, free from fear and worry. It reminds me of when Jesus was asleep in the boat in the middle of a storm whilst the disciples were very much afraid. They woke Him "Teacher, do you not care that we are perishing?"[2] When we lie down, we shall not be afraid and our sleep will be sweet. We have a peace of mind and we are able to lay our heads down at night time and rest assured. God has given us a sound mind and a peace to know He is in control, even as we sleep.

2 Tim 1:7 (NKJV)
For God has not given us a spirit of fear, but of power and of love and of a sound mind.

Fears can often disturb our sleep and affect our ability to switch off. Fear is not a gift from God, exactly the opposite – our fears are the fiery darts of the enemy, looking for an unguarded door into our subconscious. Well, not today Satan!

On the other hand, there is such a thing as a healthy fear of God. A reverence for the One who can speak all things into existence. A fear that keeps us accountable for our actions and words, because of a desire to please the Saviour.

Lord, let the only fear I have, be a healthy fear of you. Help me have peace in my mind so that my sleep can be sweet and unaffected. I relinquish control and cast my burdens onto you, in Jesus name, Amen.

June 28th – *One Touch*

Y1 – Deut 5 & 6 / Y2 – Isa 25 & 26

Mark 5:25-29 (NKJV)
Now a certain woman had a flow of blood for twelve years and had suffered many things from many physicians ... When she heard about Jesus, she came behind *Him* in the crowd and touched His garment. For she said, "If only I may touch His clothes, I shall be made well." Immediately the fountain of her blood was dried up, and she felt in *her* body that she was healed of the affliction.

I could not get in touch with one of our precious ladies from church. She had physical and mental health conditions, and lived alone in a cold and lonely three-bedroom house. The COVID-19 lockdown was the perfect scenario to cause her immense distress, so after calling for days I started to panic. I reached out to a couple of her friends and they were experiencing the same problems I was.

My husband and I decided to go visit her and found her looking very frail, something obviously wrong. We spoke to her, but received little to no response. She just stared at the floor and occasionally uttered a few words accompanied with some hand gestures. It seemed she was going through a complete mental breakdown. There's only one thing you can do in that situation, pray! Oh my, did we pray!

She looked like she needed to be held and shown some love. But how? We were in the middle of a pandemic and shouldn't have even been there! In the end, I thought 'stuff it' and gave her a big hug, a nice long squeezy one. Immediately, I felt her relax and she looked somewhat relieved. When we saw her a few days later, by a miracle she was back to her normal self! Did that touch make a difference? Jesus' healing power and a loving hug made all the difference.

This text tells us that a touch from Jesus brings connection and healing. *Are you in need of a fresh, supernatural touch from God?* Take time to connect to Him and you'll never be the same.

James 4:8 (NLT)
Come close to God, and God will come close to you ...

June 29th – *Watch Out!*

Y1 – Deut 7 & 8 / Y2 – Isa 27 & 28

2 Samuel 20:9-10 (NKJV)
Then Joab said to Amasa, "Are you in health, my brother?" And Joab took Amasa by the beard with his right hand to kiss him. But Amasa did not notice the sword that was in Joab's hand. And he struck him with it in the stomach, and his entrails poured out on the ground; and he did not strike him again. Thus he died ...

Joab met Amasa with a friendly greeting, showing respect, making him comfortable, and putting Amasa off his guard. David had appointed Amasa as commander of his armies, replacing Joab, so Joab killed him out of rivalry and concern that Amasa did not genuinely support David.[1]

Not every friendly face has your best interests in mind. We can fall away from the Lord through other people close to us because, over a period of time, we get comfortable and let our guard down without even realising. Sin will disguise itself and pretend to be harmless, but it is the ultimate destroyer. 'Sin will take you farther than you want to go, keep you longer than you want to stay, and cost you more than you want to pay.'[2] We must always keep our guard up!

The wife of a minister is no exception! *How's your prayer life?* Jesus often told His disciples to, 'Watch and pray.' *What about daily time in the Bible?* Jesus was able to withstand the lies and temptations of the enemy with the Word. *Have you allowed your heart and mind to dwell on things that it shouldn't?* In the church or workplace, there will always be people who teeter on the edge of gossip or slander. *Do you allow yourself to listen or be swayed, allowing for a crack in your armour?*

1 Peter 5:8 (NKJV)
Be sober, be vigilant; because your adversary the devil walks about like a roaring lion, seeking whom he may devour.

Peter tells us we must be alert and diligent. Keeping your eyes on Jesus will help you recognise the danger in situations before it is too late.

June 30th – *Study & Sermon Notes*

Y1 – Ps 51 / Y2 – Jer 5

Thank you for reading The Devotional Life of a Pastor's Wife

Our prayer is for God to continually stir your heart and give you a fresh ability to minister with effectiveness and joy. But as this volume draws to a close, we are aware that the ministry can take its toll on the best of us. This can sometimes result in a crisis of faith that is difficult to talk about. If you find yourself in this position, we want to reassure you that you belong to a Saviour who loves you today as much as the day you first received Him, and it is possible to start again. Here is a prayer of repentance for the woman whose heart has gone astray.

Father, I come before you today and acknowledge my sin. I repent of all unrighteousness and I am asking you to take lordship over my life and give me the strength to change. I believe that Jesus died and rose again on the third day and in faith I receive your forgiveness and salvation. I surrender my heart and future into your hands. Thank you, in Jesus name, Amen.

We encourage you to speak to your pastor, husband or trusted spiritual friend about the decision you have made today. God's mercies are renewed every day and his love for you endures forever.

CONTACT US

pwdevotional@outlook.com
(Need a friend or want to share your story)

WEBSITE

www.pwdevotion.co.uk
(Free complete Bible in one year/two years PDF)

BOOK RECOMMENDATIONS

Autobiographical
Bruchko – Bruce Olsen
Chasing the Dragon – Jackie Pullinger
Hungry for More of Jesus – Rev David Wilkerson
Run Baby Run – Nicky Cruz
Seeking Allah, Finding Jesus – Nabeel Qureshi
The Cross and the Switchblade – Rev David Wilkerson
Tramp for the Lord – Corrie Ten Boom

Financial
The Money Secret – Rob Parsons

General
Armed and Dangerous: The Ultimate Battle Plan for Targeting and Defeating the Enemy – John Ramirez
Case for Christ: A Journalist's Personal Investigation of the Evidence for Jesus – Lee Strobel
Deadly Emotions – Don Colbert
Deliverance to Dominion: How to Gain Control of Your Life – John Gooding and Joseph Campbell (Christian Fellowship Ministries)
Disciplines of a Godly Woman – Barbara Hughes
Fresh Wind, Fresh Fire – Dean Merrill and Jim Cymbala
Gay Girl, Good God: The Story of Who I Was, and Who God Has Always Been – Jackie Hill Perry
How to Win Friends and Influence People – Dale Carnegie
Knowing God – J I Packer
Let Me Be A Woman – Elisabeth Elliot
Lies Women Believe and the Truth That Sets Them Free – Nancy Leigh DeMoss
Living a Life of Fire – Reinhard Bonnke
Mere Christianity – C S Lewis
More Than A Carpenter – Josh McDowell and Sean McDowell
Power Through Prayer – E M Bounds
Still Taking The Land – Wayman Mitchell and Greg Mitchell (Christian Fellowship Ministries)
Why Standards? – Jay Nembhard (Christian Fellowship Ministries)
Zeal Without Burnout – Christopher Ash

Marriage
Devine Design: God's Complementary Roles for Men and Women – John F MacArthur
His Needs, Her Needs – Willard F Harley Jr
Sacred Marriage – Gary Thomas
The Legacy of a Couple – Ruth and Billy Graham
The Proper Care and Feeding of Husbands – Dr Laura Schlessinger
The Surrendered Wife: A Step-By-Step Guide to Finding Intimacy, Passion and
It's Not Supposed to be This Way– Lysa Terkeurst

Pastor's Wives
Sacred Privilege: Your Life and Ministry as a Pastor's Wife – Kay Warren
The Minister's Wife: Privileges, Pressures and Pitfalls – Ann Benton and Friends
The Pastor's Wife – Sabina Wurmbrand

Raising Children
Aren't They Lovely When They're Asleep– Ann Benton
Bring up Boys – Dr James Dobson
Bringing up Girls – Dr James Dobson
Dare to Discipline – Dr James Dobson
Glow Kids: How Screen Addiction is Hijacking Our Kids – And How to Break
In Praise of Stay-at-Home Moms – Laura Schlessinger
The Strong Willed Child – Dr James Dobson

APPENDIX

April 5th – Desire Wisdom
1- Strongs Dictionary, Bible Hub, 2004-2020, Accessed 08/2020 https://biblehub.com/greek/4678.htm

April 10th – Day & Night
1- https://sermons.faithlife.com/sermons/63448-meditate

April 11th – Psalm Sunday
1- Zechariah 9:9

April 16th – Navigating Emotions
1- Oxford Dictionary, Lexico, accessed 07/2020
https://www.lexico.com/en/definition/objective

April 17th – Memory Loss
1- Exodus 20:8
2- 1 Corinthians 11:24
3- Deuteronomy 32:7
4- Luke 17:32
5- Deuteronomy 15:15
6- Colossians 4:18
7- Psalms 77:11

April 20th – Subtle Resentment
1- Title: Resentment, what does it mean at having been treated unfairly and what causes it? 28/08/20
https://www.thetappingsolution.com/what-is-resentment/#:~:text=The%20definition%20is%20bitter%20indignation%20at%20having%20been,combines%20the%20feelings%20of%20fear%2C%20anger%2C%20and%20disappointment.

April 23rd – No Penalty
1- https://biblehub.com/greek/2631.htm

April 27th – Historical Women
1- Corrie Ten Boom House, The History of the Museum, 2020, accessed on 20/09/2020
https://www.corrietenboom.com/en/information/the-history-of-the-museum
2- Wikipdia, Corrie Ten Boom, 2020, accessed on 20/09/2020
https://en.wikipedia.org/wiki/Corrie_ten_Boom
3- Biography, Corrie Ten Boom, 2020, accessed on 20/09/2020
https://www.biography.com/activist/corrie-ten-boom
4- PBS The Question of God, Corrie Ten Boom, 1972, accessed on 20/09/2020
https://www.pbs.org/wgbh/questionofgod/voices/boom.html

May 1st – Jehovah Nissi
1- Names of God- N.Stone pg 113 2010 edition

May 3rd – Avoiding Contention
1- Merriam-Webster Dictionary, https://www.merriam-webster.com/dictionary/contentious

May 7th – Forgive...Repeat!
1- Matthew 6:14-15
2- Matthew 18:21-35

May 14th – Tight Grip
1- Oxford Dictionary through Lexico, 2020, https://www.lexico.com/en/definition/drift
2- Oxford Dictionary through Lexico, 2020, https://www.lexico.com/en/definition/neglect

May 28th – Shimmering Saint
1- Oxford dictionary 28.08.20 definition of sanctified

May 30th – Have Discretion
1- Cambridge Dictionary, 2020 https://dictionary.cambridge.org/dictionary/english/prudence
2- Dictionary.com, 2020 https://www.dictionary.com/browse/discretion

June 1st – Jehovah M'Kadesh
1- Stone, N, Names of God, 2010 edition, page 117
2- Stone, N, Names of God, 2010 edition, page 119
3- Stone, N, Names of God, 2010 edition, page 128
4- Stone, N, Names of God, 2010 edition, page 126 & 127

June 6th – Scrolls & Parchments
1- https://www.lifehack.org/articles/lifestyle/10-benefits-reading-why-you-should-read-everyday.html
2- https://en.wikipedia.org/wiki/Standing_on_the_shoulders_of_giants
3- Proverbs 11:14

June 8th – Light's On
1- Proverbs 22:1

June 14th – Open Doors
1- Growing Christians Ministries, The Open Door, accessed 05/09/2020 https://www.growingchristians.org/devotions/the-open-door/#gsc.tab=0
2- Ellicott's & Matthew Henry's commentaries, BibleHub, 2004-2020, accessed 05/09/2020 https://biblehub.com/commentaries/revelation/3-8.htm
3- Woman of Noble Character, Open Doors, accessed 05/09/2020 https://www.womanofnoblecharacter.com/open-doors-bible/

June 15th – Mystery Revealed
1- John 16:13 NKJV

June 16th – Testimony
1. 1 Corinthians 9:22
2. Jeremiah 29:11
3. 1 Timothy 6:6

June 18th – Clean Crib
1- https://en.wikipedia.org/wiki/Ox
2- https://study.com/academy/lesson/oxen-facts-lesson-for-kids.html

June 19th – Emotionally Intimate
1- Robert J Morgan, 2020, accessed 28/08/2020
https://www.robertjmorgan.com/devotional/song-of-solomon-the-bibles-pre-marital-counseling-course/

June 22nd – Historical Women
1- https://en.m.wikipedia.org/wiki/Lilias_Trotter

June 25th – God's Medicine
1- Psalms 28:7

June 27th – Sweet Sleep
1- https://www.ncbi.nlm.nih.gov/pmc/articles/PMC5353813/
2- Mark 4:37-39

June 29th – Watch out!
1- Enduringword, 2020, accessed on 29/08/2020
https://enduringword.com/bible-commentary/2-samuel-20/
2- Quote by R Zaccharias, goodreads, 2020, accessed on 31/08/2020
https://www.goodreads.com/quotes/746709-sin-will-take-you-farther-than-you-want-to-go

I John 1:4 (NKJV)
And these things we write to you that your joy may be full.

Printed in Great Britain
by Amazon